Welcome to
The Ultimate Guide to Internet Security

Are you worried about computer viruses? Have you ever received a suspicious email and wondered what to do? Do you want to ensure your kids are safe online? Then this guide is for you.

THE INTERNET IS AN integral part of daily life. We use it for staying in touch, browsing the web, shopping, playing games and endless pursuits besides. Unfortunately, as we all know, the internet isn't always a safe place. There are criminals out there, determined to defraud you, rip you off and even take over your computer for their own nefarious purposes.

Across eleven chapters, this guide will explain everything you need to know about keeping yourself, your loved ones and your computer safe. We'll show you how viruses work; how to protect your privacy on Facebook; how to use banking and shopping sites safely; how to secure your home network against intruders; how to choose a security suite; how to prepare for a computing disaster; how to protect smartphones and tablets; and much more besides.

All of this information comes direct from the experts at *PC Pro* – but you don't need to be an expert to benefit from it. On these pages we provide screenshots, walkthroughs and clear explanations of all the important concepts, with a comprehensive glossary at the end. The only assumption we'll make is that you're using Microsoft Windows – and even then, the majority of the advice and information in this volume applies equally to Apple computers as well.

Whatever questions you may have about internet security, we're certain you'll find this guide useful – and we hope you'll enjoy reading it too.

Darien Graham-Smith, Technical Editor, PC Pro

Contents

VIRUSES AND TROJANS

Online threats come in many guises, but perhaps the most insidious dangers – and certainly the most infamous – are viruses and Trojans. In this chapter we explain what these are, what the differences are between them, how they spread and where they come from. We explore the dangers of allowing your PC to become infected, and give practical advice on how to minimise your exposure to these online nasties. And if you're worried your PC might already have succumbed, we describe the giveaway symptoms of a virus infection, and explain how to remove a virus or Trojan from your PC.

PHISHING AND FAKE WEBSITES

Online criminals don't just use viruses and Trojans to deceive – they'll also make use of forged emails and copycat websites, designed to trick you into revealing confidential information such as banking details. It's called "phishing", and it's a threat you should be aware of if you want to stay safe online. In this chapter we'll explain how phishing works – and we'll also demonstrate the clues that can warn you when an email or website isn't the real deal. If you think you might already have been the victim of a phishing attack, we'll also give you some practical advice on what to do next.

STAYING SAFE ON FACEBOOK

From students to senior citizens, Facebook is a terrifically popular site for sharing content, arranging events, playing games and simply staying in touch. Unfortunately, it's also an easy way for scammers and thieves to discover information that you might prefer kept private. In this chapter we'll explain the risks of sharing on Facebook, and give you a guided tour of its privacy settings so you can ensure your updates are read only by those you trust. We also discuss some general best-practice principles for keeping your accounts and identity safe on this and other similar sites.

BANKING AND SHOPPING

It's always important to keep your online accounts secure and private, to protect you from fraud and other criminal activity. That applies especially when you're logging on to banks, online stores or payment services. Here it's not only your personal information that's on the line, but real money, so it's more important than ever to maintain your security, and to be alert to the possibility of being scammed. In this chapter we explain some appropriate security practices for banking and shopping sites, provide advice on online payments and show you a few tips for using auction sites safely as well.

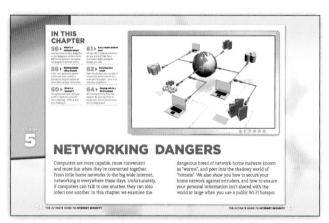

NETWORKING DANGERS

Computers are more capable, more convenient and more fun when they're connected together. From little home networks to the big wide internet, networking is everywhere these days. Unfortunately, if computers can talk to one another, they can also infect one another. In this chapter we examine the dangerous breed of network-borne malware known as "worms", and peer into the shadowy world of "botnets". We also show you how to secure your home network against intruders, and how to ensure your personal information isn't shared with the world at large when you use a public Wi-Fi hotspot.

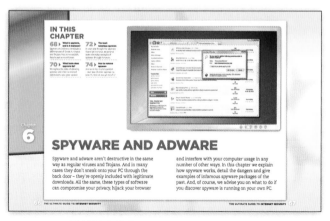

SPYWARE AND ADWARE

Spyware and adware aren't destructive in the same way as regular viruses and Trojans. And in many cases they don't sneak onto your PC through the back door – they're openly included with legitimate downloads. All the same, these types of software can compromise your privacy, hijack your browser and interfere with your computer usage in any number of other ways. In this chapter we explain how spyware works, detail the dangers and give examples of infamous spyware packages of the past. And, of course, we advise you on what to do if you discover spyware is running on your own PC.

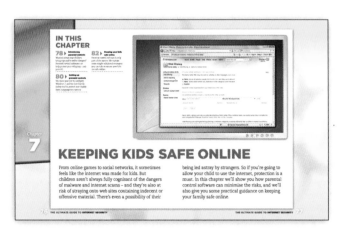

IN THIS CHAPTER

Chapter

1

VIRUSES AND

Online threats come in many guises, but perhaps the most insidious dangers – and certainly the most infamous – are viruses and Trojans. In this chapter we explain what these are, what the differences are between them, how they spread and where they come from. We explore the dangers of allowing

TROJANS

your PC to become infected, and give practical advice on how to minimise your exposure to these online nasties. And if you're worried your PC might already have succumbed, we describe the giveaway symptoms of a virus infection, and explain how to remove a virus or Trojan from your PC.

THE FIRST STEP TO KEEPING SAFE IS UNDERSTANDING THE THREATS THAT ARE OUT THERE – THEY'RE MORE VARIED THAN YOU MAY REALISE.

What are viruses and Trojans?

WE'VE ALL HEARD of computer viruses. For most of us, these nasty little programs have been causing trouble for as long as we've had PCs. Whenever a computer malfunctions, there's a good chance the finger of blame will be pointed at a virus. And it's a role that's firmly entrenched in popular culture – as far back as the 1996 Hollywood blockbuster *Independence Day*, the hero used a computer virus to infect and shut down the attacking aliens' systems.

When we talk about viruses in this way, we're using the word in a loose sense, to refer to malicious software of all sorts. But if you want to keep your PC safe, it's important to realise that, to computer experts, the word "virus" describes only one specific type of threat. There are many other dangers out there – hiding away on web servers or lurking on USB flash drives – that aren't, strictly speaking, viruses, but which can still ruin your day.

We'll cover all of these in the coming chapters, but for now we'll focus on "classical" viruses – those that meet the original, technical definition of a virus – and on another very common type of threat, popularly known as a Trojan.

WHAT IS A VIRUS? A virus is a computer program that makes copies of its own program code, enabling it to spread like a disease. The best way to explain the process is by example: one of the first viruses to hit the headlines was the SCA virus, which appeared in 1987 and targeted the Commodore Amiga system. It lodged in the computer's memory whenever the system was started from an infected floppy disk, and from that point on, it quietly wrote copies of itself to other floppy disks that were inserted into the computer's disk drive. Borrowing a single infected disk from a friend could thus lead to your own disk collection being thoroughly infected by the SCA virus.

This particular virus was comparatively harmless. All it did was occasionally surprise the user with a jokey message from the "Swiss Cracking Association" who created the virus, declaring facetiously that "your Amiga is alive!"

Unfortunately, not all virus creators have been so good humoured. Since the early 1990s, viruses have appeared on many computer platforms that deliberately attempt to destroy files, or even wipe disks completely. In a few cases virus authors

There are a huge number of different threats out there, and many different types of threats – all of which are popularly referred to by the umbrella term "virus".

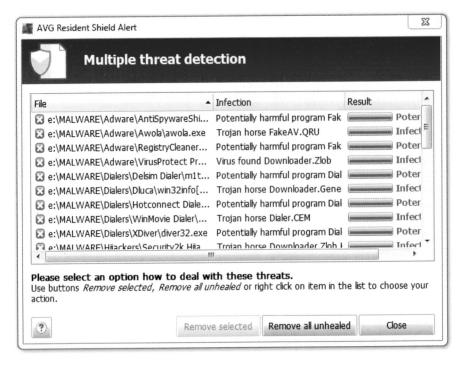

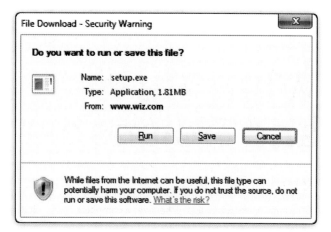

File Download - Security Warning

Do you want to run or save this file?

Name: setup.exe
Type: Application, 1.81MB
From: **www.wiz.com**

[Run] [Save] [Cancel]

While files from the Internet can be useful, this file type can potentially harm your computer. If you do not trust the source, do not run or save this software. What's the risk?

It's important to heed the warnings, and think carefully before you download software – especially from an unknown site.

have tried to extort money from victims to make their data accessible again – so called "ransomware" attacks. We'll discuss the full range of dangers overleaf, and some possible explanations for the virus writers' motivations; but for now let's just say you don't want to expose your PC to the imagination of a virus writer.

Protection against viruses is therefore essential for anyone who values the safety and security of their computer. However, it's important to remember that viruses aren't the only threat you need to look out for. Indeed, as we'll explain on the follwing pages, these days viruses ought to be comparatively low on your list of concerns.

WHAT IS A TROJAN? A Trojan is a similar type of threat to a virus. Like a virus, a Trojan lodges unseen in the memory of your PC and does its nefarious business in secret. You don't want a Trojan on your PC any more than you want a virus.

The difference is how the infection spreads. Virus infections typically come from running an infected program, or booting your system from an infected disk (see p12). Once your system is infected, the virus code then sets about subverting other programs or disks into vehicles for infection.

Trojans work differently. Rather than attempting to covertly distribute their code, Trojans disguise themselves as legitimate programs. For example, a malicious website might advertise a free trial of a popular game. Many visitors to the site will probably be tempted to download and run the installer, not realising that the the download contains a dangerous executable that will infect their computer. If the creator is cunning, the download will also include a real trial of the game, which launches once the Trojan has infected the system, so to the user the download appears legitimate. They may even go on to share the installer with others, helping the Trojan author infect even more computers. We'll cover this in more detail on the following pages.

It's probably clear now why Trojans are so called. They're named after the Trojan horse of legend – a betrayal disguised as a gift.

DRIVE-BY DOWNLOADS A classical Trojan relies on what's called "social engineering" to spread (it basically means exploiting human nature). There's a second category of threats which are sometimes also referred to as Trojans, but which work in a slightly different way.

A common or garden Trojan might work by trying to trick you into downloading and running a particular file from a particular website. This second type of Trojan works by using technical measures to trick your *web browser* into downloading and running

Let's just say you don't want to expose your PC to the imagination of a virus creator

a file, without your permission or knowledge. When this works, it's called a "drive-by download".

The attraction of the drive-by download approach to malware creators is obvious. There's no need to worry about persuading the user to download the malicious file, and because there's normally no outward sign that anything's happened, the user is less likely to get suspicious and start checking their system for possible infections.

The big limitation of drive-by downloads is that they can only work by taking advantage of weaknesses in the web browser's security (so-called exploits). The developers of all the major web browsers issue regular security updates to close off exploits as they're discovered, so malware distributors have to stay one step ahead of the browser developers – or they have to satisfy themselves with infecting only people who haven't updated their browsers. With a social-engineering approach, things are easier for the bad guys: it's difficult for a browser or security program to stop you from downloading and running malware if you're convinced you want to do so.

One tell-tale sign that you might be downloading a Trojan is if the installer asks you to disable your antivirus software, typically claiming it will "interfere with the installation". Needless to say, we strongly recommend you do no such thing!

IF YOU AREN'T CONCERNED ABOUT WHAT A MALWARE ATTACK COULD MEAN FOR YOU, YOU SHOULD BE – THE CONSEQUENCES COULD COST YOU TIME AND MONEY.

The risks of exposure

IT'S EASY TO BE BLASÉ about the dangers of malware. Statistically speaking, even if a virus or Trojan does make it onto your system, it's unlikely you'll suffer any serious loss. You may not even notice a problem. But that's no reason to be complacent. There are plenty of reasons why infection is best avoided: here are some of the main ones, in rough order of severity.

POOR PERFORMANCE Many types of malware, once they've infected your PC, run constantly in the background, looking for opportunities to spread or perform some other malicious task. Even if they never manage to do so, they're eating up memory and CPU resources which would otherwise be available for your own programs. This can noticeably degrade your PC's performance, especially for older systems with limited RAM and processing power. Startup times may be longer too, as the malware initialises.

Even on a newer PC, some malware will interfere with access to your hard disk or external drives. This could manifest as slow disk operations, or even jerky playback if you're watching a movie or listening to music.

DANGER TO OTHERS Many types of malware are infectious, so whenever a virus is running on your PC there's a risk you'll pass it on to others – and expose them to all the hazards on this page. It isn't kind to endanger your friends and colleagues in this way. Even if you're unconcerned about your own data, keeping your system clean is a courtesy to them.

It's also worth noting that some types of malware use your PC for antisocial activities such as distributing spam or phishing emails (see Chapter 2). In this case you probably won't know the people who are being inconvenienced, but it's happening nevertheless. It's simply good citizenship to ensure you're not a part of this type of activity.

DISRUPTION Malware can interfere with your computer in unexpected ways. For example, a Trojan might deliberately hijack your web browser, in a bid to keep you away from certain sites and prevent you from installing software (typically malware-removal software!). In 1999 and the early 2000s, multiple malware attacks forced corporate email systems offline, causing mayhem for many businesses. If you're trying to get an important piece of work done to a deadline, this sort of interruption is the last thing you need.

Malware can also cause problems by accident. Virus creators don't have the time or the inclination to test their creations against every possible system, so some poorly coded

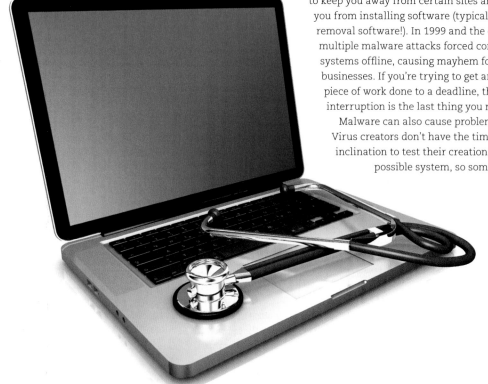

attacks end up causing Windows to become unstable, or preventing applications from working properly. Resolving problems like this can be a real pain – after all, malware isn't designed for easy removal!

DATA LOSS From the days of the earliest computer viruses, malware creators have had an unholy fascination with wiping data from their hapless victims' machines. In a few notorious cases, the virus has stored a copy the data in an encrypted form, which can be recovered if you pay for a decryption key. But this entails a certain risk to the creator – if he sets up a system for receiving payments from his victims, that provides law enforcement agencies with a possible avenue for tracking him down.

So it's no surprise that most viruses and Trojans that set out to wipe your data are purely destructive. They won't bother trying to extort money: they'll simply erase your files beyond any hope of recovery. The good news is that threats like this represent only a minority of malware – after all, there's nothing in it for the virus creators. But the risk hasn't gone away completely, and if you're hit by an attack like this, you will at least end up wasting time as you restore your lost files from a backup. If you don't have a backup, you're out of luck.

UNEXPECTED PHONE BILLS These days only a minority of us use telephone dial-up access to get online. But if you do have a modem connected to your PC, beware of a nasty little class of viruses and Trojans known as "dialers". These programs wait until the dead of night, then use your modem to call foreign premium numbers, running up enormous bills at your expense – to the benefit of the shady types who run the phone lines. Though this hazard may be dying out as the world switches to broadband connections and wireless routers, similar tricks still work with mobile phones – see Chapter 11.

IDENTITY THEFT One of the biggest threats associated with modern malware is identity theft. It's easy to understand how this works. Once a malicious program is installed on your PC, it simply sits and watches as you visit all sorts of personal websites

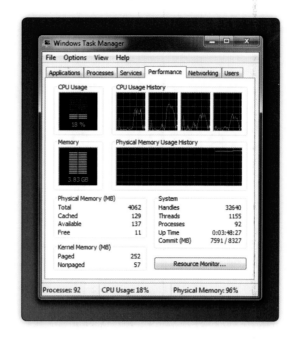

Excessive CPU and RAM usage can be just one unwelcome symptom of a virus infection.

such as Facebook and Amazon. The malware can monitor the passwords you enter, and keep a record of the information that comes up on screen. All of these details can then be transmitted to wherever the

> *Malware can monitor the passwords you enter, and record information that comes up on screen*

malware's creator chooses. The next thing you know, someone's taking out credit cards in your name – after all, they know all your personal details – and using them to buy expensive items. Under current UK law, you shouldn't be liable for the cost, but sorting out the mess is a slow and painful process, and your credit rating may take a hammering.

Things get even worse when you consider online banking. Most banks have safeguards in place to prevent crooks logging in as you and emptying your account; but it can still be very inconvenient to have your account frozen without warning.

ESPIONAGE AND CYBER-WAR It may sound like science fiction, but malware attacks have already been successfully used to steal secrets from corporations and governments. In 2011 a virus named Stuxnet was even used to successfully sabotage Iran's nuclear programme. For home PC users these issues will (hopefully) be a non-issue, but they're worth bearing in mind if you're ever tempted to write off the malware threat as overblown.

(!) Viruses can mess with your files, but it's very uncommon for them to have any effect on your hardware. If your monitor goes blank, or your keyboard stops working, it's more likely to be a hardware problem than malware.

▶ MALWARE DOESN'T SPONTANEOUSLY APPEAR ON YOUR COMPUTER – IT HAS TO COME FROM SOMEWHERE. UNDERSTANDING THIS CAN HELP YOU AVOID INFECTION.

How do viruses and Trojans spread?

THERE'S AN OLD SAYING in computer security: the only truly secure computer is one that's kept in a locked room, disconnected from all networks, and switched off. That may sound like a joke, but it's no exaggeration. Computers are inherently vulnerable things, and more or less any way you choose to use one will expose you to some possibility of infection.

That's not to say all activities are equally risky, however. In practice, there are a limited number of common ways for a virus to get into your system – a limited number of "attack vectors", in the industry parlance. If you're aware of these most likely routes for malware to infect your PC, you can take steps to protect yourself against most attacks.

HOW VIRUSES SPREAD A virus is a self-contained program that spreads by creating copies of itself. The challenge for the virus writer is getting the program run in the first place – and then to ensure these copies will themselves in turn be executed. Clearly users can't be relied upon to open unknown programs, so viruses typically try to exploit situations where the computer runs code automatically.

INFECTED BOOT SECTORS The classic attack vector for a virus is the boot sector of a floppy disk, as described on p8. The boot sector is the very first part of the disk, and typically contains basic instructions for loading the operating system (the name derives from the image of the computer "pulling itself up by its bootstraps").

By adding malicious code to the boot sector, it's possible for a programmer to lodge a virus in the computer's memory before the operating system is loaded. This virus can then monitor the disk drive and write the virus code to any other floppy disks that are subsequently inserted.

Back in the days when kids exchanged pirated computer games in the school playground, a boot sector virus could spread like wildfire across dozens of machines. Today, very few computers even have a floppy disk drive, meaning boot sector infections are effectively a thing of the past. In principle, it's possible for a virus to infect a hard disk in this way – but since people don't tend to move their hard disks back and forth between computers, there's very little scope for the infection to spread.

EXPERT TIP ▾
Because of the way viruses replicate, infections can hang about for years on forgotten flash drives or in disused email archives. In many cases older malware won't work with modern applications and operating systems, but don't assume programs and files are safe just because they're outdated.

An act as innocent as plugging a USB flash drive into your computer could expose you to infection.

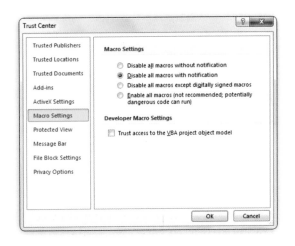

As a defence against macro viruses, Microsoft Office applications default to strict security settings.

INFECTED PROGRAMS One limitation of boot sector viruses is that the user has to boot from the disk in order to be infected. "File viruses" get around this by infecting not disks but individual program files. This is achieved by finding an executable program on the host PC and inserting extra virus code into it. Whenever the program is next run, the virus will be installed into memory. To allay suspicion, the program will then continue to execute as normal.

File viruses have been around for many years, and like boot sector viruses their heyday is probably past. These days the software on our PCs tends to come directly from original installation media, or from fresh downloads directly from the publisher, so there's little chance of our stumbling across an infected application.

DOCUMENTS AND PDFS Viruses don't have to be standalone programs. In the mid-1990s, soon after Microsoft started adding macro capabilities to its Office applications, it became apparent that these capabilities could be used to create a virus that lived inside a document. For example, a user might create a Word document that launched an embedded macro as soon as it was opened. This macro would then automatically duplicate itself into all subsequent documents that were opened.

The potential of this approach was demonstrated by the Melissa virus in 1999, which not only infected Word and Excel documents but also used scripting features in Outlook to mass-mail copies of itself to the first 50 addresses in the user's contacts list. Mayhem ensued: the total disruption to businesses who had to shut down email systems and disinfect users' PCs was valued at more than $80M.

Microsoft has now updated Office so that macros no longer run automatically, shutting down that particular attack vector. But other types of document can still be dangerous: in recent years malware creators have found ways to insert viruses and Trojans into PDF files, so you can get infected simply by viewing a document. The only defence against attacks like this is to keep your software up to date (including antivirus software), and be wary of documents that come from untrusted sources.

AUTOPLAY When Microsoft introduced Windows XP it débuted a revolutionary new feature called "AutoPlay". The idea was simple: whenever you inserted a shiny CD-ROM or DVD-ROM disc into your PC, the disc's menu or installation screen would automatically pop up, without your having to click around and launch it manually. It was a simple idea that added a note of slickness to the operating system.

Unfortunately, it was also an idea that was open to abuse. CD-ROMs are immune to virus

There are a limited number of common ways for a virus to get into your system

infection, since they can't be written to. But virus creators soon realised that it was possible to write malicious AutoPlay information onto USB flash drives.

A slew of AutoPlay viruses followed, all of which spread in the same way: whenever you plugged an infected flash drive into your PC, the virus would automatically load into memory, and thereafter proceed to infect any other flash drives you might subsequently use. External USB hard disks were vulnerable too. With USB media fast replacing floppy disks as the standard way to share files, it was a textbook virus epidemic.

Microsoft has partially addressed the problem in Windows XP SP3 and subsequent editions of the operating system. Now, whenever a new disc or flash drive is inserted, a menu pops up asking whether you want to use AutoPlay or access the disk in some other way. This makes it harder for the infection to spread; but we suspect there are still a large number of infected flash drives lurking out there from the bad old days. Unless you've a very good reason to say yes to AutoPlay, we suggest you steer clear.

(!) On these pages we describe the most common ways of getting infected, now and in recent years. But new attack vectors keep being discovered, so don't assume that being aware of all these tricks is enough to keep you safe.

Be suspicious of emails that arrive out of the blue from unknown senders – and all the more so if they have attachments.

EMAIL ATTACHMENTS AND LINKS Once upon a time, spam was just a nuisance, filling up your inbox with unwanted adverts. Nowadays it can be actually dangerous. Some spam includes web links that are designed to trick you into giving up your personal information – this is called "phishing", and we'll talk about it in detail in Chapter 2.

Non-phishing emails can be dangerous too. Document-borne viruses and Trojans, of the type we discussed above, often spread by email: typically the message will appear to come from someone you know, and it will contain an attachment such as a Word document or a PDF file, with an innocent looking message such as "hey, what do you think of this?". If you open or run the attachment, you'll be infected.

Sometimes the attack will come in the cruder form of an executable file mailed directly to you. Most mail clients will warn you of the dangers before opening executables received over email, but if the virus writer is clever they may use trickery to persuade you that the file is legitimate.

One common deception is to take advantage of the default setting in Windows that hides filename extensions – that is, the last three letters of a filename that tell you (and Windows) what sort of file you're dealing with. With this setting enabled, a file called "DOCUMENT.EXE" will appear in Windows Explorer under the name "DOCUMENT". This can be exploited for devious purposes by sending out files with names like "DOCUMENT.DOC.EXE". This will appear on your computer as "DOCUMENT.DOC" – in other words, it will look like a harmless Word document.

BUNDLED INSTALLATIONS Sometimes, when you download a "free" game or tool from a legitimate website, you'll find it wants to install extra components – components that have nothing to do with the program itself, but which are included purely for the purposes of advertising or sponsorship. It's an open question whether these unwanted components really qualify as "malware", because they install overtly – they don't try to hide away in your system – and they can normally be removed via the Control Panel. Arguably, such bundling may even be a good thing, as the fees software creators are paid to package these little programs in with their own wares helps to fund the future development of free software. Unfortunately, they can often be a nuisance, and some of them they may even qualify as "spyware" (see Chapter 6).

BITTORRENT If you've ever wondered how pirated games and movies spread, the answer is mostly via BitTorrent, a networking system that makes it easy to share any sort of software and files semi-anonymously. BitTorrent allows anyone on the network to download whatever files they want from anyone else in the world who already has them. It's a clever system, which eliminates the need for a single download server.

Unfortunately, no central server means no central quality control. When someone accidentally shares a file that's infected with a virus or Trojan, that file may well then go on to be shared with thousands or millions of other users. There's no way to fix it or recall it: the genie's out of the bottle. It's no surprise, therefore, that BitTorrent is also used by criminals as an avenue for deliberately seeding new malware into the wild, by attaching it to desirable content.

The best defence is to steer clear of BitTorrent altogether. The network does, however, have legitimate uses: for example, it's a convenient way to distribute very large, publicly available files such as Linux installation discs. Even if you're downloading a file like this, however, be cautious, as there's no guarantee that what you're downloading is the original, uninfected file from the publisher.

FAKE DOWNLOADS Fake downloads – that is, downloads which promise something desirable, but which actually simply infect your PC with malware – are the regular *modus operandi* of Trojans. They're similar to infected BitTorrents, but in this case the infected software is normally served up directly from a plausible-looking server. The source may even be a legitimate and respectable download site, which has simply been tricked into hosting the malware, so to avoid them you must cultivate a healthy distrust of *all* downloads.

A fake download may come in more or less any guise – it could be presented as a free game, an update for a piece of software you already own or an innocuous toy such as a screen saver. One common deception is the fake video codec. The trick works by showing you a web page with a YouTube-style video box, or a download link, typically promising a funny, shocking or sexy video. Click to view it and you'll be told you need to download and install a codec – a "coder and decoder" module – to watch the video. If you agree, however, and run the downloaded file you won't get access to the video: you'll just get infected.

Another common trick is the fake antivirus scam (*illustrated right*). Typically this starts with a web page popping up a warning along the lines of "a virus has been detected on your PC!" You'll then be prompted to buy and install an antivirus package to remove the infection. In reality the infection may never have existed – the warning was just a ruse to scare you into spending money on an "antivirus" package that does nothing.

Sometimes the infection is real, and you'll be plagued by warnings and popups until you succumb and buy the software – or until you remove the infection using a reputable antivirus package.

FAKE ANTIVIRUS

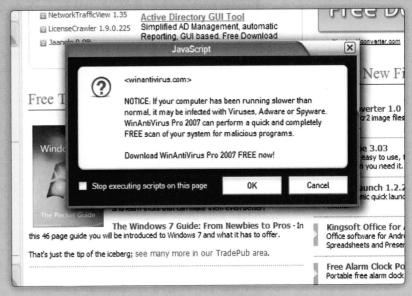

The first you'll know of a fake antivirus scam is when you're browsing the web and a pop-up warning appears claiming your PC might be infected. It's likely this warning will come from a page that has nothing to do with viruses, so it'll come as a bolt from the blue – the intention is, after all, to alarm you. Naturally you'll want to take advantage of the offer of a free virus scan, so you can assess the seriousness of the situation.

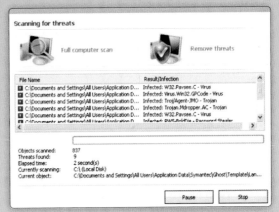

The "scan" may take the form of a download that infects your PC. It will then "detect" one or more viruses that – it claims – conventional antivirus software can't remove. In reality, reputable security software can easily deal with such threats.

If you pay for the suggested "antivirus" software, the warnings will indeed go away. But effectively you've just paid the scammers to put an infection on your PC and then remove it again – and you've also handed them your credit card details.

▶ UNDERSTANDING THE PEOPLE BEHIND MALWARE – AND THEIR MOTIVATIONS – CAN HELP YOU TO ANTICIPATE WHAT THE THREATS MIGHT BE.

Malware authors may not all dress like cat burglars, but their work is just as shady.

Who creates viruses and Trojans?

THERE ARE LITERALLY millions of viruses, Trojans and other threats out there in the wild, so we must be wary about making sweeping statements about where they all come from. But the majority of malware is created and distributed by just a few types of people.

RESEARCHERS AND HOBBYISTS Some viruses are created for fun, or out of intellectual curiosity, to see what's possible and for the challenge of finding ways around computer security systems. Certainly this was the case with the earliest viruses, which were often designed to do nothing more malicious than spreading themselves as far and wide as possible. Nowadays, however, it's well understood that even this can have a hugely destructive effect (by overwhelming internet servers, for example) and researchers are strongly discouraged from testing their skills in this way.

SPIES AND SABOTEURS We mentioned earlier that malware could be used for political purposes, and there's plenty of evidence to suggest that it's already happening. Naturally, no government will publicly admit to creating viruses and planting them on foreign computers, but forensic analysis of various viruses and Trojans suggests that eastern and western intelligence agencies are already trying to use

malware to spy on each other and disrupt operations. In just the same way, malware can be used as an unofficial business tool for stealing corporate secrets. It's even suspected that some governments are using malware within their own borders to disrupt political dissident movements.

CYBERCRIMINALS Believe it or not, most of the malware that's likely to infect your home PC is a product of organised crime. Creating a virus capable of evading the defences of a modern operating system demands a very high level of technical skill, so an entire "black economy" of programmers who will create viruses on a paid-for, freelance basis has emerged. In some cases programmers have even formed sophisticated development teams, complete with quality assurance and testing processes to ensure their malware can't be easily detected or blocked. The malware is then purchased or leased by middlemen, who use it for their own purposes such as harvesting credit cards or sending spam.

Geographically, many of these malware creators appear to be based in Eastern Europe, Russia, Brazil, India and China. It's surely no coincidence that these are all regions with weak or unbalanced economies, providing strong incentives for talented programmers to get involved in criminal activity.

► THERE ARE MANY WAYS TO CATCH MALWARE, BUT THERE ARE ALSO PLENTY OF MEASURES YOU CAN TAKE TO REDUCE THE RISK.

How to avoid viruses and Trojans

BY NOW IT SHOULD BE OBVIOUS that you don't want to get a virus – not that there was ever much doubt on that count. However, with criminals constantly seeking new ways to sneak their infections onto your PC, there's no single measure you can take to ensure you'll stay safe. Take note of these basic principles, however, and you'll greatly reduce your chances of being caught out by a virus.

TRUST NO ONE It's sad but true: on the internet, you can't trust anybody. When a suspicious email, web link or file lands on your system, even if it comes from a friend or family member, you can't take its *bona fides* for granted. For a start, it's quite possible that the sender has already been infected by a virus without realising it, and could be unwittingly about to pass it on to you. Or, a virus might have hijacked a friend or work colleague's email account, and could be sending out infected messages without his or her knowledge – we've seen plenty of attacks that do just this.

There's simply no way to be sure, and just one slip can expose you to an infection. Under the circumstances, a policy of "better safe than sorry" is well advised. If you receive a link or an email attachment you weren't expecting, you might even

consider making a quick phone call to the originator, to check they really meant to send it to you.

STICK TO REPUTABLE SOURCES If you like to download music, videos or games, you'll know there are thousands of websites to choose from. But it's a good idea to stick with the most official sources you can: either the publisher's own website, or services such as iTunes for music and Steam for games.

Such precautions reduce the risk that your download, or the website it comes from, will have been infected with malware. After all, a download on the publisher's website will have been supplied from within the company, so you can have a high level of confidence that it hasn't been tampered with. You can't be quite so sure when you're downloading the file from a no-name shareware site based in Moldova.

Big names also have big budgets, and big reputations to protect. This means they're motivated and able to invest in preventing security breaches, and on reparing them should the worst come to pass. We're not saying the likes of Amazon and Apple are immune, and we're certainly not saying all smaller websites are riddled with malware. But as a matter of best practice, bigger sites tend to be safer.

EXPERT TIP ▼

Some people think Linux systems and Apple Macs are immune to viruses. This isn't actually true: Apple's OS X has been the target of several attacks in recent years. However, these systems are less vulnerable than Windows, and there are fewer viruses that target them. Overall, Apple and Linux users are less likely to get infected.

Love or hate iTunes, there's one thing that has to be said for it: it's unlikely to give you a virus.

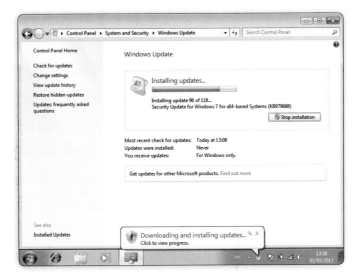

Control Panel ▸ System and Security ▸ Windows Update

Control Panel Home

Check for updates
Change settings
View update history
Restore hidden updates
Updates: frequently asked
questions

Windows Update

Installing updates...

Installing update 96 of 118...
Security Update for Windows 7 for x64-based Systems (KB979688)

Stop installation

Most recent check for updates: Today at 13:08
Updates were installed: Never
You receive updates: For Windows only.

Get updates for other Microsoft products. Find out more

See also

Installed Updates

Downloading and installing updates...
Click to view progress.

**Keeping your operating system and applications up to date is crucial
if you want to protect your PC from malware.**

SHARE ONLINE We mentioned
on p12 that boot sector viruses have
all but died out because people no
longer share floppy disks. But modern
removable media such as USB flash
drives and external hard disks can still
carry viruses, which could infect a PC
as soon as the drive's connected. If you
want to share a file with someone, it's
safer to send it by email, or use sharing
features in a service such as Dropbox
(www.dropbox.com). This greatly reduces the risk of
any nasties coming along for the ride.

QUESTION UNEXPECTED BEHAVIOUR Viruses
and Trojans almost always try to get onto your
system without your full awareness. This can lead to
odd behaviour, giving away the fact that something
suspicious is going on. For example, be suspicious
if you see unexpected popups
asking questions like "are
you sure you want to run this
program?" – these tend to
indicate that something is trying
to surreptitiously install itself,
and they should be denied.

USE UAC AND STANDARD ACCOUNTS
Windows' User Account Control (UAC) feature is an
obstacle to malware: it prevents running programs
from accessing your Windows settings and program
files – and hence getting their claws into your system –
unless you click to give your express permission.

Some people find these requesters intrusive,
however, and turn them off. This is a bad idea: with
UAC disabled, a virus can install itself completely
silently. We understand that UAC can be a pain,
especially when you're setting up a new PC, installing
applications and customising the desktop. But once
that's done, in everyday use, you'll almost never see
UAC, so it's a very good idea to re-enable it.

Similarly, it's a good idea to check in the User
Accounts section of the Control Panel to see whether
you're logging in with an Administrator account or
a Standard one. If you're an Administrator, consider
creating a new, Standard account for everyday use.
When you're logged in with a Standard account,

programs will need to ask your permission before
making any sort of change to the system, giving
you yet more opportunity to prevent malware from
inveigling its way onto your system.

UPDATE YOUR SOFTWARE Virus writers are
always looking for new vulnerabilities in Windows
which can be exploited. Make a point of running
Windows Update regularly, to close off these

> *Make a point of running Windows Update
> regularly, to close off vulnerabilities*

vulnerabilities. Ideally you should set Windows to
download and install updates automatically, but this
can be annoying as Windows will periodically insist
on restarting to finish the installation process.

Don't neglect your applications, either. As
we've mentioned, viruses have been known to hide in
Word documents and PDFs, and vulnerabilities in your
web browser can provide an easy route for Trojans to
get onto your system.

To be safe, it's best to keep all the programs on
your PC up to date. Many applications offer a built-in
a "Check for updates" option, and third-party update
checkers such as UpdateStar (www.updatestar.com)
can help too.

INSTALL ANTIVIRUS SOFTWARE The single
most effective thing you can do to protect yourself
from malware is to install antivirus software, which
will automatically detect and remove malware as
soon as it lands on your system. See Chapters 8 and
9 for our complete guide to nine of the best security
packages available.

Windows
XP is more
vulnerable
to malware than
Windows 7, 8 or
Vista, as it lacks
some important
security features,
including UAC. If
you're still using
XP, upgrading to
Windows 7 or 8 will
make you safer – if
your PC can run it.

HOW TO...
TELL IF YOU HAVE A VIRUS

Viruses, Trojans and other malware come in many different forms – but these are some general telltale signs of infection.

1 ▶ **YOUR COMPUTER FEELS SLOW**
As we mentioned on p10, a slow computer isn't necessarily an indicator of an infection: more often than not it just means you have too many programs running in the background. But if your PC suddenly slows down for no apparent reason, that could be a sign that a virus has made its home on your hard disk.

2 ▶ **YOU CAN'T DELETE SOME FILES**
A classic symptom of virus infection is when you find a file on a USB drive that you don't recognise and try to delete it – only to find that you can't! Either the virus is preventing you from removing it, or it's automatically re-infecting the disk as soon as it sees the original infection has been removed. Again, though, this isn't proof positive that you've been infected: Windows itself will prevent you from deleting some types of file, such as those needed for running applications.

3 ▶ **YOUR PC CRASHES OR FREEZES**
Modern malware is often designed to stay "under the radar", so it can do its dirty work for as long as possible. That means viruses won't normally crash your PC on purpose. However, if you've kept Windows and all your applications up to date, many viruses will hopefully find themselves unable to work in the intended way and will fail. This could cause your system to become unstable, or to freeze completely – a clue that something fishy is going on.

4 ▶ **NEW ICONS ON YOUR DESKTOP**
Some viruses are used in money-making scams, which work by encouraging infected users to visit advertising sites. Sometimes these are quite brazen: for example, you might see a new icon appear on your desktop saying "Click here for sexy pictures!" This is a sure sign that something's been meddling with your PC – unless you created it yourself, of course.

HOW LONG?
If you're concerned, it only takes a minute or two to check for common symptoms.

HOW HARD?
There's very little to it – just check a few programs are working as they should and remember to keep an eye out for anything unexpected.

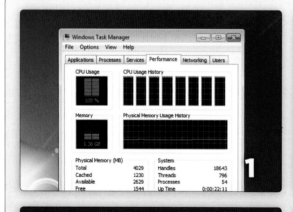

5 ▶ YOUR BROWSER IS HIJACKED

It's not just icons that try to steer you towards the criminals' preferred websites. Many viruses and Trojans will change your browser settings, so that an unfamiliar home page appears when you open it. They may also try to add toolbars to your browser: these can spy on your activity (see Chapter 6) or simply provide yet more ways to send you to the desired sites. If anything about the appearance or behaviour of your browser changes suddenly, or if it pops up an unexpected requester asking you to confirm a change of settings, that's a red flag for a potential virus infection.

6 ▶ UAC AND FIREWALL WARNINGS

We mentioned UAC on p19 – the feature that prevents programs from accessing sensitive system files without your permission. The Windows Firewall does a similar thing, preventing unknown programs from accessing the network (something they might do to try to infect other computers). If you see an access request from either UAC or the Windows Firewall, that suggests something is trying to infect your PC – or that something already has.

7 ▶ BOUNCED EMAILS

If you log in to your email one day and find it's full of "bounce" reports – that is, messages warning that an email you sent couldn't be delivered – that's cause for suspicion. This is typically what you'll see if a rogue virus on your PC has been trying to mail out copies of itself. (The bounces happen because most people's address books contain numerous old addresses that are no longer valid.) Some viruses are clever, though, and supply a fake "From:" address on the emails they send – so it could be that it's not you but someone else you know who's infected.

8 ▶ CAN'T INSTALL WINDOWS UPDATES OR RUN ANTIVIRUS SOFTWARE

Malware writers hate Windows Update, and they *really* hate antivirus software. So the first thing many viruses and Trojans do is disable these services, so they can go about their nasty business in peace. If you can't run Windows Update, or if you can't open your regular antivirus software, that's a strong hint that something on your system doesn't want you patching vulnerabilities or scanning for malware.

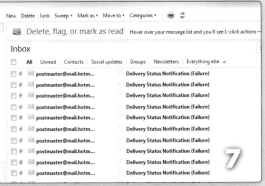

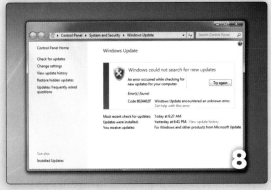

EXPERT TIP ▼

In theory, you ought to know right away when you have a virus – because your antivirus software ought to warn you! But with the best will in the world it's simply not possible to create a virus scanner that can recognise every possible threat as soon as it appears. So it's still a good idea to keep your eyes open for possible infection symptoms.

▶ A VIRUS INFECTION NEEDN'T BE THE END OF THE WORLD: IT'S OFTEN POSSIBLE TO
RESTORE AN INFECTED SYSTEM TO FULL WORKING ORDER.

What to do if your PC is infected

NO MATTER HOW MUCH care you take, sooner or later it's possible your computer will be infected. If it happens, don't blame yourself: some criminals dedicate their entire careers to finding creative and undetectable ways of circumventing computer security: you'd need a degree in computer science and a whole lot of luck to avoid them all.

And don't panic too much about the fallout. Most malware infections can be cleaned up without damaging your system: see our guide opposite to disinfecting your PC. There are, however, a few important things you should do once the malware has been removed.

CHANGE YOUR PASSWORDS As we mentioned on p11, many malware attacks are intended to steal passwords and other personal information. Not all of them have this aim, but if your PC's been compromised it's safest to assume the worst. Even if you haven't seen any suspicious activity on your online accounts, it's possible that your passwords have been spied on and may be abused in the future. We recommend that you change as many of them as

is practical at your first convenience – and at the very least you should change the password to your primary email account. If you don't, it's not just your personal correspondence that's compromised. An attacker could easily go to a site such as Amazon or Facebook, click the "I Forgot My Password" link, then intercept your email to gain access to your accounts.

CONTACT YOUR BANK If your PC is used for online banking, there's a chance your account details could have been compromised. Check your bank's website for any guidance, or give them a call, as there may be certain procedures you need to follow. See also our advice on p32 for what to do if your bank details are stolen in a "phishing" attack.

TELL YOUR FRIENDS Viruses spread. If you've got a virus, there's a good chance you might have passed it on to a friend – or, perhaps you caught it from a friend who still doesn't know he has it. As a courtesy, we suggest you warn anyone who's been exchanging files or links with you that they might have been exposed to malware.

**EXPERT
TIP** ▼
Some security
experts take the
view that once a
computer's been
compromised it
can never be fully
trusted again. That
may be overkill
for your own PC;
but if a virus does
manage to infect
your system, that's
probably a sign
that it's time to
audit your security
provisions. How did
the malware reach
your PC? And could
it happen again?

Dealing with any
compromised
passwords should
be an urgent priority,
especially if you've
used the same
password for more
than one service –
see p42 and p52.

HOW TO...
REMOVE A VIRUS

1 ▶ **PERFORM A FULL ANTIVIRUS SCAN**
Hopefully you already have antivirus software installed on your PC. If so, simply open the interface and start a complete scan of your system. Don't just perform a quick scan, as this may miss malware that's hidden away in program folders or email archives. It's also a good idea to plug in any USB drives you own, to ensure they're scanned too. When the scan's complete, you should see a full report of all malicious objects found, and – depending on the software you use – various options of what to do with them.

2 ▶ **START YOUR PC FROM A BOOT CD**
If Step 1 doesn't seem to solve your problem, or if you don't have antivirus software installed, try performing a scan from a CD-based boot environment. This can be more effective than running a scan from within Windows as it prevents the malware from interfering. There are several free boot CDs available for download: one popular one is the AVG Rescue CD, available from www. avg.com. To use it you'll need a CD or DVD writer, and a blank optical disc. Follow the instructions, then boot from the CD when you're ready to scan.

3 ▶ **RUN SYSTEM RESTORE**
On the rare occasions when a virus gets lodged so deeply into your PC that it can't be removed, Windows' System Restore feature may save the day. To access it, open the Start menu in either Windows Vista or Windows 7 and type "System Restore". You'll see a list of recent changes that were made to your system: click "Show more restore points" to see ones from more than a few days ago. Choose one, click "Next" and your PC will be reverted to that state – although your personal documents won't be touched, so you won't lose recent changes.

4 ▶ **REINSTALL WINDOWS**
If the virus is somehow managing to cling on even after you've run System Restore, you may have to resort to a fresh installation of Windows. If your PC came with a recovery DVD or partition, it's safe to use this – but back up your documents first, as they'll be lost. If you're reinstalling from a regular Windows DVD, boot directly from the disc, to ensure the virus can't interfere, and perform a clean installation – don't reinstall over the top of an infected system!

HOW LONG?
A scan takes mere minutes, but using System Restore or reinstalling Windows can take up to an hour.

HOW HARD?
If you want to take hands-on measures to restore your system to a pre-virus state, you'll need a certain degree of confidence and technical knowledge.

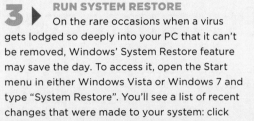

IN THIS CHAPTER

Chapter

2

PHISHING AND

Online criminals don't just use viruses and Trojans to deceive – they'll also make use of forged emails and copycat websites, designed to trick you into revealing confidential information such as banking details. It's called "phishing", and it's a threat you should be aware of if you want to stay safe online. In

FAKE WEBSITES

this chapter we'll explain how phishing works – and we'll also demonstrate the clues that can warn you when an email or website isn't the real deal. If you think you might already have been the victim of a phishing attack, we'll also give you some practical advice on what to do next.

NOT ALL ONLINE THREATS COME IN THE FORM OF MALICIOUS SOFTWARE. PHISHING WORKS IN A TOTALLY DIFFERENT WAY TO VIRUSES, BUT IT'S JUST AS DANGEROUS.

What is phishing?

IN THE LAST CHAPTER we discussed the workings of viruses and Trojans. These are what you might call "traditional" malware: they take the form of malicious software running on your PC, typically without your knowledge, and you can minimise your exposure to them by preventing unrecognised programs from running on your PC.

Unfortunately, malware isn't the only threat. Using a technique called "phishing", criminals may still be able to steal your sensitive information without using a single piece of software – except your regular email client and web browser. In this chapter we'll explain how it works, and how you can defend yourself against it.

FAKE EMAILS AND WEBSITES Ordinarily, your first exposure to a phishing scam will be an email that arrives out of the blue, apparently from your bank. It will probably look authentic, and not particularly suspicious. A typical phishing message might say simply: "We're updating our records. Please log in to your account within the next 48 hours and check that your details are stored correctly on our database." The email will also contain a helpful link that will open the bank's login page directly in your browser, so you can check your account right away.

Needless to say, this link is bogus. It may look like a genuine link to your bank, and the odds are that if you click it you'll be taken to a page that looks exactly link your bank's real login page. But in reality this is a fake. The criminals have created a replica of your bank's website, hosted on a server which they control. The intention is to get you to enter your banking details, which the crooks can then use to transfer money out of your account.

Phishing is an insidious threat, because there's no simple defence against it. It doesn't require any software to run on your PC, so systems such as UAC and the Windows Firewall can't prevent it. Your email client and antivirus software can try to warn you when a suspicious looking message arrives – but since every phishing email is different, they're hard for a computer to spot reliably. It can be difficult even for a well informed human to spot a phishing email, as the perpetrators make use of some clever deceptive tricks to make their emails and websites seem genuine.

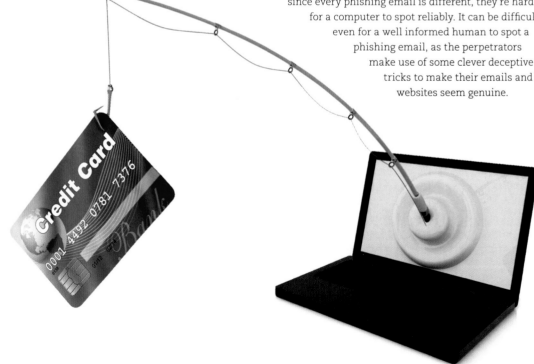

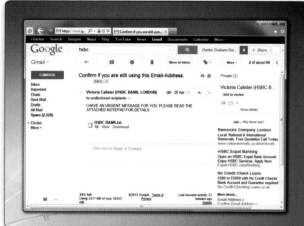

A phishing scam may start with a reasonable-sounding request, such as this one asking us to confirm our contact details.

PERSONAL INFORMATION Phishing relies on lulling you into a false sense of security, so crooks try to make their approaches appear as genuine as possible. For example, they may include your personal name in the email, to suggest that it's come from someone you have legitimate dealings with. (This may also help the email get past any junk filters in your email system, as it will look more like a real email, and less like generic spam.) In reality, the sender may have got this information from any number of sources: it's quite likely that you yourself have made your name and address public on a website, a blog or an online service such as Facebook.

Even if you haven't shared your details, they can still fall into criminals' hands. Perhaps your name and email address fell into the wrong hands when a friend of yours, who has your name and email address stored on their PC, caught a virus. Phishing attacks can also make use of personal information that's been stolen from online services, such as discussion forums. It only takes one hacker to break into a service and leak the user database, and your name, email address and who knows what other information is out there for anyone to exploit.

While the phishers may put some effort into getting your name right, they quite often send emails purporting to be from the wrong bank. Obviously this is a dead giveaway: if you're a Lloyds TSB customer, an email asking you to log into your Santander account is going to look very suspicious indeed. But it's actually quite tricky for scammers, who are probably based in another country, to find out who you bank with, since this information is much more rarely shared online. So they simply send the same message to everybody on their list, assuming that enough people will see the right bank, and will be taken in, to make the scam worthwhile.

AUTHENTIC APPEARANCES Assuming the phisher has managed to pick the right bank, it's vital that the email and website look authentic, so as not to arouse suspicion. Typically the email you receive will

include the real logo of the bank – copied directly from the bank's website, of course – and it may well include all sorts of other genuine content, such as information links and adverts for financial services, copied and pasted from a real bank email. If you're skimming through your messages, this can provide an effective veneer of plausibility.

The only thing that can't be wholly authentic is the link which takes you to the login page, as this must lead you to the fake website rather than the

The intention is to get you to enter your banking details, which the crooks can then use

real one. This may be far from obvious, though: due to the way weblinks work, all you're likely to see in your email client is a line saying "click here to log in", or even a graphic. You may therefore not realise anything's wrong until you click on the link and visit the phishing site.

A BELIEVABLE WEBSITE A phishing site is likely to look very much like your bank's real login page. Again, the criminals can easily copy and paste the content from the real site, complete with all the expected graphics and links, so there's no reason for anything to look conspicuously out of place. That said, some phishing attempts are quite shoddy, with typographical errors and missing or wrongly placed graphics. Hopefully if you come across a site like this you won't be tricked!

Although phishing sites can be unnervingly accurate, there are a few suspicious signs that you can check for immediately if you think something fishy might be afoot. We'll detail several of these signs on p30, but perhaps the most important anti-phishing

Phishing isn't limited to computer communications: one variant that's doing the rounds involves someone phoning you up, claiming to be from Microsoft technical support. If you get a call like this, be warned – it's a scam!

tip – and one of the simplest – is to look at the web address of the site, shown at the top of your browser. For example, if you're expecting to log in to an HSBC account, check that the domain name of the page is www.hsbc.co.uk. If it is, that's a good sign that the page is real (though not a guarantee, as we discuss below). If the domain name is something suspiciously unfamiliar – perhaps with an unusual country code at the end, such as pages001.konnect3.ua – it's very likely you're being phished.

DOMAIN NAME DECEPTIONS An obviously dodgy domain name can indicate a phishing attempt, but the converse isn't always true. It's more or less impossible for phishers to get a fake login page hosted on a real bank domain: this would require a tremendous lapse in security on the part of the bank. But they do sometimes use domains which look, at a glance, very similar to the correct ones. For example, a scammer might host a phishing site at www.lloydtsb.co.uk (note the subtle typo). Or, one might take advantage of the visual similarity between the number "1" and a lower case "l", and use www.11oydstsb.co.uk.

Phishers can also mislead their victims by inserting reputable-sounding names into their web addresses. The important thing to remember is that it's the *last* part of a web address – not including the ".com" or ".co.uk" – that confirms the "domain". Anything to the left of this is a "subdomain", which can be anything the domain owner likes. So if you're visiting www.barclays.co.uk, the page you're seeing is owned and controlled by Barclays. But if the page address is www.barclays.scam999.co.uk, it has nothing to do with the bank – it's operated by whoever owns the "scam999.co.uk" domain.

A final trick phishers can employ to disguise their web addresses is to use foreign characters. This doesn't mean using foreign addresses: obviously if you're expecting to log in to the Nationwide Building Society and you find yourself diverted to скамсайт.рф, that's going to arouse suspicion.

Rather, they take advantage of the visual similarities between different alphabets. The Russian address above, for example, contains an "a" character that's indistinguishable from the western letter "a". If you were to register the domain "nationwide.co.uk", using a Cyrillic "a" as the second letter, it would look

just like the real Nationwide domain, but it would be entirely under your control. This trick hasn't yet been widely used, but it's a dangerous prospect, as it's impossible to detect with the naked eye. This means sometimes you'll have to rely on other methods for spotting fake sites, as we describe on p30.

THE GOLDEN RULE OF PHISHING On the following pages we'll show you several ways to recognise phishing emails and websites, and what you can do if you are taken in. But there's one simple measure you can take to make yourself immune to phising attacks: create a bookmark in your browser that leads to your bank's real website, and always use this bookmark to log in rather than following links. This way you can never be led astray. Unfortunately, human nature being what it is, this isn't as easy as it sounds – phishing emails are designed to get you to click, and you only need to let your guard down briefly to be tricked.

EXPERT TIP ▼

If you use the Firefox browser, consider installing the free Petname extension, which is available from addons.mozilla.org. This handy tool automatically shows you a note to confirm when you return to a site you've marked as trustworthy – and warns you when you end up at an untrusted one.

HOW TO...
SPOT A PHISHING EMAIL

1 ▶ SUSPICIOUS ADDRESSING

Phishing mails typically come with an inconspicuous sender name such as "Natwest Bank customer support" – but the email address that's associated with this name may be more revealing. Scammers rarely use the bank's real email address, as this would cause undelivered messages to bounce back to the bank's actual customer services department, alerting them to the scam. If you receive an email where the sender's email address doesn't seem to match the purported sender – for example, if the domain is wrong – that suggests it's a phishing attempt.

2 ▶ A CALL TO ACTION

Phishing scammers really want you to click on their fake links, so they'll try all sorts of tricks to encourage you to do so. The message in a phishing email might say you've won a prize which can only be claimed by clicking. Or, it might say there's a problem with your account, and you need to log in within a time limit to resolve it – creating a sense of urgency in the hope you'll act quickly and incautiously. Be wary of anything that seems to be pushing you to click the login link.

3 ▶ INCONGRUOUS ELEMENTS

Many scammers don't speak English as their first language, so phishing emails sometimes contain glaring grammatical mistakes that give the game away. Scammers also don't have the resources of an international bank when it comes to design and testing: when you view a phishing email in your mail client, there's a good chance the scammer's message and login link may be visually inconsistent with those parts of the email copied from a real bank communication. Watch out for text which is larger or smaller than it ought to be, or in the wrong font or colour.

4 ▶ A DECEPTIVE LOGIN LINK

Some phishing scams include a login link that's presented as a bare web address – the intention being to reassure you that it leads to a safe and familiar site. Click on it, however, and you might well be whizzed away to somewhere totally different. Always check that the page you've ended up on is the same as the one promised in the email. There's no legitimate reason why it shouldn't be, so if you've been misdirected it's almost certainly a sign of foul play.

> (!) Phishing emails are often sent to huge numbers of people at once: if an email is addressed to "undisclosed recipients", that could be a sign of a phishing attempt too – though it's possible your bank is simply being discreet.

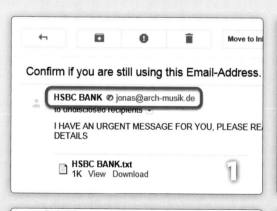

HOW TO...
SPOT A FAKE WEBSITE

Look out for these subtle – and not so subtle – signs that the site you're using might not be entirely trustworthy.

1 ▶ **BROWSER WARNINGS**
All major web browsers have built in technology that will warn you when you visit a site that's known to be fraudulent. This protection isn't perfect – new sites spring up every day, so the absence of a warning isn't a guarantee of safety. But if your browser does alert you that the site you're visiting isn't to be trusted, take its advice seriously and get the hell out of there.

2 ▶ **SOMETHING LOOKS WRONG**
Technically, it's not hard for scammers to create a perfect-looking copy of your bank's website. But often, through either incompetence or laziness, they'll leave out graphics, features or links which you, as a regular customer, expect to be there. Sometimes they won't even bother with a full website, and will simply produce a basic password entry form or a pop-up window. Trust your instincts: if the site you're using doesn't "feel" right, back out.

3 ▶ **WRONG ADDRESS**
Fake websites can often be identified by dodgy web addresses. As we mentioned on p28, phishers use tricks to disguise suspicious addresses, including some which are undetectable to the naked eye – so don't assume that, just because the address looks right, you're in the right place. But if your bank's login page appears to move from natwest. com to 4234-net.cn, alarm bells should be ringing.

4 ▶ **INSECURE CONNECTION**
Banks use secure, encrypted connections for their login pages, to ensure your details can't be observed by intruders. You can identify a secure connection by the code "HTTPS" which appears before the web address. Check your browser for this code before entering your password. If you see only a regular "HTTP" connection, or nothing at all, don't enter your details: the connection isn't secure and the page is almost certainly not kosher.

HOW LONG?
It only takes a few moments to look over a web page and check for suspicious elements.

HOW HARD?
The technology behind secure connections and web certificates is quite technical, but you don't need to know the details of how they work – just what to look out for.

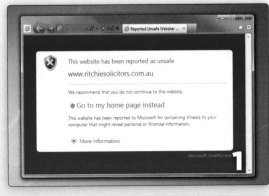

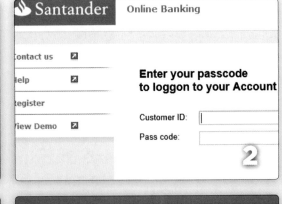

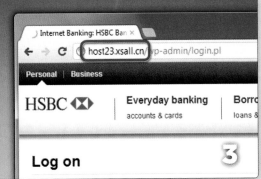

5 ▶ CHECK THE CERTIFICATE

Banks and payment services like PayPal don't just rely on secure connections: they also use high security web certificates to confirm their identity (see p50 for an explanation of certificates). The certificates used by most reputable online services appear as a green bar in the web address field in your browser, confirming the name of the company that owns the page. These certificates are all but impossible to forge, so if a website presents a green certificate you can be very confident that it's a real bank or service. Conversely, if a website lacks a certificate – especially a site that you'd expect to see one, such as a bank – it's probably fake.

6 ▶ WANTS TOO MUCH INFORMATION

When you log in to your bank, it may only ask for a few numbers from your passcode. This is a deliberate policy – it's done so that intruders can't learn the entirety of your login information by watching you log in once. If you're suddenly asked for your entire passcode, or for other seemingly unrelated information such as the PIN code to your debit card, that's a very suspicious sign.

7 ▶ NO SITEKEY

SiteKey is a system that confirms you're logging into a trusted site by showing you a piece of information that only that site ought to have access to – typically a graphic and a phrase chosen by you. If your bank uses SiteKey, this information should be shown every time you log in. It's not a perfect system, because if a fake login process simply skips over this step, you may not notice its absence. But if you do realise that your SiteKey information hasn't been shown at the appropriate time, consider it a serious warning. For more on this, see p47.

8 ▶ CAN'T ACCESS YOUR ACCOUNT

Phishing sites are just fronts, with no actual connection to your bank; so once you've entered your credentials, they won't be able to show you any details of your account. Instead, you might see a page claiming the site is down for maintenance, or you might be returned unceremoniously to the login prompt. If you didn't realise it already, this unhelpful behaviour is an after-the-fact clue that you've been phished. Time to take remedial measures, as detailed overleaf.

EXPERT TIP ▼

If you fancy putting your ability to recognise fake websites to the test, there are several free online quizzes available. Certificate authority Verisign hosts a popular fake website recognition quiz at www.phish-no-phish.com. Once you've mastered that, try the quiz at www.opendns.com/phishing-quiz.

> IF YOU'RE TAKEN IN BY A PHISHING ATTACK, DON'T HESITATE: ACT QUICKLY AND YOU MAY STILL BE ABLE TO PROTECT YOUR ACCOUNTS AND FINANCES.

What to do if your details are stolen

When you realise you've just entered your banking details or passwords into a fake website, you're likely to get a sinking feeling. But if you act quickly you can mitigate the damage, before the criminals have a chance to make use of their ill-gotten information.

CHANGE YOUR PASSWORDS If you've been tricked into revealing a password to a phishing site, you should change it on the real site as soon as possible, so that scammers can't log in as you. This is particularly important for online payment services such as PayPal and Google Checkout: these services aren't covered by normal banking regulations, so you might not be able to recover any money that's fraudulently transferred out of your account.

CANCEL CREDIT CARDS If a phisher has obtained your credit card details, contact the card issuer right away using the hotline for stolen cards (the number should be printed on the back of your card, and advertised prominently on the issuer's website). Don't dawdle: you can't be held liable for any transactions that take place after you report the fraud, but if you give the crooks time to make a big purchase then any refund will be at the discretion of your card issuer.

NOTIFY YOUR BANK Each bank has its own approach to stolen information: yours might apply extra security measures to your account, or change your credentials so the compromised ones are no longer valid. Call them quickly: you'll be doing them a service by alerting them to a phishing attack, and notifying them may again limit your liability.

TELL THE POLICE Phishing is a crime: if you've been a victim, consider filing a formal police report at www.actionfraud.police.uk. This will assist police investigations, plus it establishes an official record of events, which could be helpful if you later need to show that your details have been used fraudulently.

MONITOR YOUR CREDIT REPORT After a month or two, consider ordering a personal credit report. This will help you identify any outstanding debts that may have been run up using your details. You can then contact the creditors, explain that the debts are fraudulent and ask them to clear your name. If you don't do this, these incorrect records could cause financial trouble for you in the future. One agency that offers free credit reports for a limited period is Equifax: find out more at www.equifax.co.uk.

EXPERT TIP ▼
Someone who's willing to operate a fake website scam probably won't hesitate to infect you with a virus as well. After you've taken the steps on this page, it's worth running a quick virus scan, just to make sure that plausible-looking login page wasn't concealing a nasty Trojan.

Your bank's website will contain plenty of information on what to do if you're caught out by a scam.

IN THIS CHAPTER

Chapter

3

STAYING SAFE

From students to senior citizens, Facebook is a terrifically popular site for sharing content, arranging events, playing games and simply staying in touch. Unfortunately, it's also an easy way for scammers and thieves to discover information that you might prefer kept private. In this chapter we'll

ON FACEBOOK

explain the risks of sharing on Facebook, and give you a guided tour of its privacy settings so you can ensure your updates are read only by those you trust. We also discuss some general best-practice principles for keeping your accounts and identity safe on this and other similar sites.

▶ THE INTERNET WAS MADE FOR SHARING, BUT BE AWARE THAT THE INFORMATION YOU PUT ONLINE COULD BE TURNED TO CRIMINAL PURPOSES.

What are the dangers of Facebook?

FACEBOOK IS THE LARGEST social media site in the world, with more than 800 million active users. This makes it a great hub for connecting with old and new friends. Unfortunately, it also makes it an attractive target for criminals looking to harvest personal data and scam the unwary. In this chapter we'll look at how you can use Facebook as safely as possible; but the first step is to explore exactly what the risks are.

IDENTITY THEFT Facebook is a goldmine of personal information. Browse through someone's profile and there's a good chance you'll be able to find their full name, their date of birth, what town they live in, what school they attended, the date of their wedding anniversary and so forth. If they've connected with family members online you may be able to work out their mother's maiden name too.

Clearly this information is open to abuse. For example, armed with these details, a criminal might be able to phone up your bank and persuade them that they were talking to the real account holder. The first step to using Facebook safely, therefore, is making sure you're not sharing sensitive information with

the world at large. On the following pages you'll find a walkthrough of Facebook's security settings which should help you lock down your information.

EXPOSING YOURSELF When your timeline's full of banter from friends, it's easy to think of Facebook as a private thing – a safe place to post comments and pictures you might not want aired in public.

Just like your personal information, however, these updates may be more widely available than you think – and the consequences of sharing them can be serious. We've heard tales of employers turning down job applicants because of incautious remarks they've made online, and of public sector workers being fired or disciplined for posting material that's deemed to reflect poorly on their professionalism. As we discuss on p41, it's vital to bear in mind how your posts may appear to others.

On a more uplifting note, the possibility of revealing more than you mean to cuts both ways. At the end of 2011 a violent mugger in Darlington was sent to prison after the victim discovered his identity – by searching for him on Facebook.

As we discuss on p41,

The wealth of personal information that's given away freely on Facebook makes it an identity thief's dream.

EXPERT TIP ▼

Your Facebook account isn't quite such a juicy target as your bank account, but the information it contains can still be valuable to criminals. So it's no surprise that some phishing attacks try to trick you into giving up your Facebook username and password. Don't fall for it – always log in via the main portal.

Facebook offers no reliable way to confirm that a potential friend really is who they say they are.

YOUR FRIENDS GIVE YOU AWAY Watching your own posts may not be enough to keep your Facebook profile clean. Facebook's photo tagging picture means that, by default, anyone can take a picture of you, perhaps in a compromising position, upload it to their own profile, and associate it with your account – so that, with absolutely no input on your part, it appears when someone searches for you. If you lead a double life – a sober-suited accountant by day, perhaps, and a party animal by night – you may well wish to restrict this feature, as we describe overleaf.

NO PROOF OF IDENTITY Even after you've secured your settings, so that only verified friends can acccess your details and see your photos, you may still be at risk – because on Facebook there's no way to be sure that all of your friends are who they claim to be. When you accept a new Facebook friend request, you're often doing so on the strength of very little information, and there's no way of verifying that even that's true.

Indeed, researchers have found that many Facebook users will accept friend requests from entirely fictitious individuals, especially if they have attractive profile pictures, or if they claim to be old classmates. These fake accounts could easily be controlled by con artists or covert investigators – and unless you make careful use of Facebook's Lists feature (see over), they'll have access to all the same personal information as your most trusted bosom buddies.

UNTRUSTWORTHY APPS One of the key features that makes Facebook more than just a message board is its support for third-party apps. The ability to play games with your friends adds a whole new dimension to social networking, but it can also be a liability.

At the very least, apps can be an irritation. App developers typically make money by showing adverts within their apps, so it's in their interest to push as many people as possible to install and use them. To this end, many apps act almost like viruses: as soon as one of your friends installs and runs an app, it bombards all of their friends with messages urging them to install the app themselves. This isn't exactly dangerous, but it's a pain.

Nuisance apps aren't the only concern. Many apps demand access to your personal information before they'll run. There's simply no way of knowing where this information is going to end up: effectively, when you run an app like this you're accepting its author as a trusted friend. Unfortunately, there have been numerous reports of malicious Facebook apps that deliberately steal personal information. Another nasty trick apps can pull is posting links to malware or phishing-type websites on your wall. Because the

> *Many Facebook users will accept friend requests from entirely fictitious individuals*

link appears to come from you personally, your friends are more likely to be tricked into clicking than if it had come anonymously like a regular phishing attack.

These concerns don't just apply to apps that run within Facebook, either. Many desktop applications and online services now come with an integrated "connect to Facebook" feature. If you authorise them to use your account, you may be giving them permission to collect your personal details and wreak havoc in your name.

CONSTANTLY CHANGING Mark Zuckerberg has said that one of the core maxims of Facebook development is "move fast and break things". True to his word, Facebook is constantly evolving, with new features appearing and old ones changing all the time.

This keeps Facebook fresh and exciting. Sadly it also means you can't just choose security settings once and then forget about them. New updates can compromise your security in unexpected ways, so if you want to stay safe you must be alert and keep on top of new Facebook features as they appear.

> ! It's easy to accumulate a long list of Facebook apps; we suggest you periodically cull any you're not regularly using. This reduces the risk of a long-forgotten app catching you off guard with unwanted behaviour.

HOW TO...
MANAGE FACEBOOK SECURITY

Facebook's settings pages offer several ways to tighten up your privacy and security. These are some of the most important.

HOW LONG?
There's a good range of settings on offer, and it's worth taking a few minutes to read through and consider them all.

HOW HARD?
To get Facebook set up just the way you want it you'll need to understand how things like tags and public posts work.

1 ▶ **LINKED ACCOUNTS**
You'll find this setting under **Account Settings ▶ General** (click the small downward arrow at the top right of Facebook). Linked accounts let services such as Google and MySpace share your information and login credentials with Facebook, so you don't need to log into each one separately. This is a handy time saver, but it means a thief can gain access to huge amounts of personal information just by stealing one password. For greater privacy, use this setting to unlink your accounts.

2 ▶ **SECURE BROWSING**
Located under **Account Settings ▶ Security**, this option tells Facebook to use an encrypted HTTPS connection whenever possible. Turning it on is a no-brainer: it doesn't affect your use of the service in any way, but it does guarantee that any would-be spies are unable to pinch your personal details by monitoring the web traffic.

3 ▶ **LOGIN NOTIFICATIONS**
If someone else were to log into Facebook as you, you'd want to know about it. This setting, under **Account Settings ▶ Security**, provides that warning. Turn it on and you'll get an email every time your account connects from a device you haven't used before. Consider also enabling Login Approvals: this blocks anyone from logging in from an unknown device unless they can enter a security code that's sent to your mobile phone.

4 ▶ **CONTROL YOUR DEFAULT PRIVACY**
On the main **Privacy Settings** page you can set a default protection level for everything you post. At the very least, check this is set to "Friends". A safer idea is to create a list of trusted friends' accounts that you know to be genuine (see overleaf): choose the "Custom" privacy setting and you can ensure that whatever you post is visible only to members of this list by default.

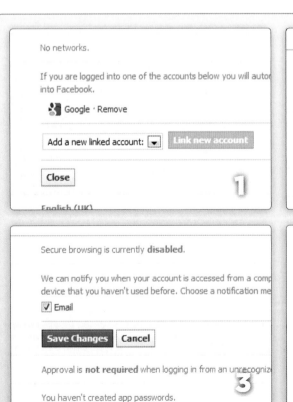

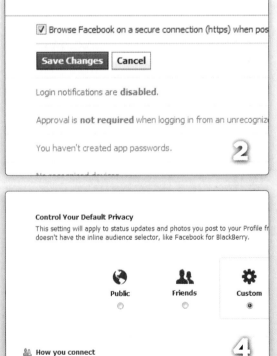

5 ▶ WHO CAN LOOK YOU UP

Your personal email address is probably public knowledge and easy to find. Much of your Facebook information is much more private, so you don't necessarily want people armed only with your email address to be able to find it. Under **Privacy Settings ▶ How you connect** you can restrict this ability to friends, or to friends of friends.

6 ▶ REVIEW TAGS

If you're carefully looking after your online reputation, you don't want careless friends undermining your efforts by tagging you in unfortunate photographs or suggestive comments. Under Facebook's **Privacy Settings ▶ Profile and Tagging** options, you can choose to review and approve tag requests from friends. You can also choose to confirm the tags that other people add to your own posts. Another interesting setting in this section relates to Facebook's facial recognition system, which will suggest your name as a tag when a friend someone uploads a picture that looks like you. If you're jealously guarding your identity, you can disable these suggestions.

7 ▶ BRINGING YOUR INFO INTO APPS

When one of your friends authorises a Facebook app to access their profile, that app doesn't just gain access to their details – it can also read what they know about you. Obviously this is a huge security loophole, but happily it's one you can close off. In **Privacy Settings ▶ Apps and websites** you can specify precisely which parts of your profile should be accessible to friends' apps, and which should be blocked. You can also click to "Turn off all apps" – the nuclear option! – or block specific people and specific apps from accessing your non-public details. You'll find this option under **Privacy Settings ▶ Blocked People and Apps**.

8 ▶ PUBLIC SEARCH

If you're still worried about the information someone might be able to extract from your Facebook account, a final measure you can take is to try to prevent them from finding it in the first place. The last option under **Privacy Settings ▶ Apps and websites** is "Public Search": disable this and Facebook will stop sharing your profile information with search engines, making it harder to track down.

3
Staying safe on Facebook

Common-sense best practices for Facebook

WE MENTIONED IN Chapter 1 that Trojans are hard to defend against with technical measures, because they trick you into deliberately trying to download and install their malware. Similarly, Facebook's privacy and security settings can't stop you mistakenly placing your trust in a persuasive criminal. No matter how strictly you've locked down your account against intruders, it's vital to keep your common sense about you whenever you're using Facebook.

GET TO KNOW THE SYSTEM Facebook is a big and complex system, and the first step to being safe is making sure you understand the dangers. In this chapter we've explained the major threats, and some ways you can protect yourself against them, but it's always a good idea to check out the site's official security advice and procedures. Your gateway to this advice is the user page at www.facebook.com/security: click from here onto "Security Homepage" and you'll find several valuable resources, including Facebook's official security guide, a blog discussing current security issues and even a quiz. If you think your account's been hacked, or if you've noticed

suspicious activity from another user, this is where you report it too: click on the "Take Action" button at the bottom of the page to see help and action links for a wide range of security-related concerns and scenarios.

BE WARY OF FRIEND REQUESTS Clearly, accepting Facebook friend requests from complete strangers is a bad idea. We suggest you steer clear, even if the stranger seems like a fun and attractive person: after all, a scammer trying to collect Facebook friends is hardly likely to create a boring, ugly profile.

If a friend request comes from someone who looks plausible, but whom you don't know well, consider having a quick chat with them before accepting, just so you can confirm that they really are who they appear to be. In fact, it's a good idea to do this with all friend requests, even ones apparently from people you know well, since you've no other way of confirming that someone's the real deal.

Finally, before accepting a friend request, take a moment to question whether the person really is someone you want to have access to your personal

Facebook's security portal is a good starting point if you've any questions or concerns.

Facebook's Lists feature makes it easy to share content with only your most trusted friends.

Facebook isn't your only way to share personal information over the internet. We focus on a few other options overleaf – but many of the suggestions on this page are good general principles for any sort of online service.

timeline. Facebook security isn't just about identity thieves, either: adding parents and work colleagues could lead to embarrassment down the line should you feel inspired to share some off-colour jokes or candid pictures.

DIVIDE FRIENDS INTO LISTS To minimise the risks of over-sharing, it's a good idea to divide your friends into lists. You can find full details of how lists work, and how to create them, at www.facebook.com/help/friends/lists. Using lists makes it easy to keep your most personal posts away from people you don't know so well – while retaining those people as friends so you can still include them in events and chat with them directly.

POST WITH CAUTION Even if you're scrupulous about who you befriend, and who gets put on what list, you should always remember that anything you post online can easily be shared more widely, even outside of Facebook: after all, how hard is it to copy and paste? The only real way to ensure your private moments, jokes and photographs remain private is is never to share them online in the first place. Sad, but true.

BE ALERT TO SUSPICIOUS BEHAVIOUR Like all passwords, Facebook passwords can get stolen or cracked from time to time. On p42 we'll discuss ways to prevent it happening to you. But what if a friend's account is broken into? The impostor will have access to all the information you've shared with that friend, and they may be able to get you to reveal far more by taking advantage of your trust. So if a Facebook friend starts sending you suspicious questions, such as asking you to confirm your home address, don't be too eager to help. Equally, if you start receiving suspicious looking web links, don't be too trusting, as the site could easily be a phishing or malware attack.

Rather, try to get hold of the account holder via some other means, to check whether it's really them sending the messages. If it's not, you'll be doing them a favour by warning them anyway, as only the account holder can reclaim a hijacked account. This can be done at www.facebook.com/hacked.

DON'T SHARE YOUR LOCATION Facebook includes location features that let you share where you are, as well as what's on your mind. It's a fun way to share your travels with your friends, but depending on where you live it could be a green light for burglars to target your house, knowing that it's unoccupied. You can find out more about Facebook's location features at www.facebook.com/about/location.

Even if you don't use Facebook's built-in features, it's a good idea to resist the temptation to

Anything you post online can easily be shared more widely, even outside of Facebook

advertise your movements in real-time. It's much safer to wait until you get home to share your experiences. And whatever you do, don't share your home address: even if thieves don't come calling in person, they can use this information, along with the other details you share, to cause all sorts of problems for you.

DON'T ADD APPS CASUALLY As we mentioned on p37, untrustworthy apps are an endemic threat on Facebook. There's simply no way to tell whether the latest app to appear on your friends' walls is legitimate, or whether it's a malicious Trojan designed to harvest your personal information.

Obviously Facebook would be a dull experience if you never used any apps. But you should resist installing every app that comes along just to see what it does, or simply because you've received a generic wall-post from a friend telling you to. Choose which apps you add carefully, and try a web search first to check other people's experiences. Once a malicious app steals your details there's nothing you can do to get them back, so it's a case of better safe than sorry.

▶ A GOOD PASSWORD OUGHT TO BE IMPOSSIBLE TO GUESS, BUT THAT NEEDN'T MEAN IMPOSSIBLE TO REMEMBER. HERE'S HOW TO GET THE BEST OF BOTH WORLDS.

Choosing a secure password is a vital step in safeguarding your online identity.

Creating a secure password

If a nasty piece of malware steals your Facebook password (or any other password) it's time to change it. But what should you change it to? If you pick something easy to remember – such as "password" or "Facebook" – there's a chance an intruder could guess it, or find it using a "brute force" computer program.

This is why many online services these days insist that your password must be at least a certain number of characters long, and must include a mix of capital and lower-case letters and numbers – something along the lines of "GZoLM8". This makes it much harder for a hacker to guess your password, even if they take millions of attempts. Unfortunately, it also makes it much harder for you to remember it.

YOU'VE GOT TO HAVE A SYSTEM One way to come up with a secure yet memorable password is to make up an abbreviation for a phrase you associate with the service. For example, you might think of Facebook as "that site I post photos to". Take the first letter of each word and you've got "TSIPPT". To make it even more secure, and to ensure our password meets the site's requirements, we might change the

case of one the letters and write the last "to" as a digit instead, giving us "TSiPP2". This password is just as secure as "GZoLM8", but much more memorable. For even better security, use a longer phrase. And when you need to change your password, simply come up with a new phrase.

PASSWORD MANAGEMENT It's a bad idea to use the same password on more than one service: cyber-criminals know people do this, so if some nefarious hacker manages to steal your Facebook password, they'll likely try it out on services like Gmail, Amazon or PayPal too.

All the same, remembering lots of different passwords is a pain. All the major web browsers will offer to remember passwords for you: this can be a big help, but be cautious if you're using a PC that someone else might have access to. Stored passwords can also be a liability if you're using a laptop that could get lost or stolen – see p127. The easiest and most secure answer is to install password management software that creates and stores passwords for you. See p52 for a guide to the popular, free LastPass system.

HOW TO...
STAY SAFE ON OTHER SITES

GOOGLE+

Google's social networking system works on similar principles to Facebook's, so much of what we've written in this chapter applies here too. One feature that's worth noting, however, is the "Share" button beneath each of your stream posts. This enables anyone who can see a post to repost it to their own circles – even if its audience was originally restricted to a hand-picked circle of friends. This means that, on Google+, you need to think more carefully still about what you share, and who you trust to read your posts, as even restricted postings are a mere mouse-click away from being shared with the wider world.

MYSPACE

These days, MySpace is chiefly used as a music networking service rather than a full-on social network. All the same, you can easily end up sharing more than you mean to with contacts. Click the small "Edit profile" link at the top right of the page and you'll see a host of settings where you can customise who can see and contact you, and block your details from being accessed by third-party apps and services.

TWITTER

With no friend requests and no apps, staying safe on Twitter is comparatively simple. A big part of it is remembering not to post anything you don't want made public, as tweets can be searched and read by anyone. Remember too that the person tweeting at you may not be who you think it is, as there's no policing to prevent people creating accounts under assumed names. A final hazard that's particular to Twitter is the problem of blind links: all web links contained within tweets are automatically shortened, so you can't see where they lead. Click with caution.

LINKEDIN

This career-oriented social network is a comparatively safe place: like Twitter it doesn't support apps, so there's no threat there, and because of the professional focus there's less temptation to share sensitive personal information in the first place. As always, though, be alert to phishing scams and dodgy links. And don't rule out the possibility that someone trying to connect to you could be an impostor, possibly hoping to discover commercially sensitive information.

> **!** Big websites like to share information, so check the T&C's carefully before you sign up for new services, or connect existing accounts together. Otherwise, information you've guarded carefully on one could "spill out" via another.

IN THIS CHAPTER

Chapter

4

BANKING AND

It's always important to keep your online accounts secure and private, to protect you from fraud and other criminal activity. That applies especially when you're logging on to banks, online stores or payment services. Here it's not only your personal information that's on the line, but real money, so it's more

SHOPPING

important than ever to maintain your security, and be alert to the possibility of being scammed. In this chapter we explain some appropriate security practices for banking and shopping sites, provide advice on online payments and reveal a few tips for using auction sites safely as well.

Secure authentication for online banking

ACCESSING YOUR BANK account is one of the most risky things you can do online. With most web services, the risk is that a criminal observer could compromise your account to access personal information, which could in turn be used to commit some kind of fraud. But if someone gets into your bank account, they can immediately start transferring money out. This is why, as we discussed in Chapter 2, banks are a common target of phishing attacks.

To reduce the risk, many banks have adopted advanced login procedures far more sophisticated than a regular username and password system. The intention is that even if someone does trick you into revealing your credentials, they still can't get full access to your account. That may sound paradoxical, but we'll explain how it works below.

The various methods we describe here are all used by banking institutions, but we're not aware of any organisation that combines them all: each bank uses its own selection of security measures. But it's still well worth being aware of the possibilities – at the very least it's useful information to have should you wish to switch banks.

FIXED, ANONYMOUS CREDENTIALS The first security measure banks use isn't terribly complicated, but it makes a big difference. It's well known that, despite the risks, many people habitually use very weak passwords such as "123456" or "letmein". Banks ensure this doesn't compromise security by assigning complex passcodes which can't be changed, effectively shutting down "brute force" hacking attacks. They may also assign unguessable user names, so that hackers can't target your account by trying variations of your personal name or email address.

PARTIAL INPUT Your passcode may be nine characters long, but when you log in a bank will typically ask for only three characters from it – perhaps the second, third and sixth. The next time, it will ask for a different selection characters. This approach is designed to frustrate password-stealing attempts: even if a so-called "key logger" Trojan manages to capture a perfect record of the credentials you entered to log in to your bank this morning, an attacker will be unable to use those same credentials to illicitly access your account this afternoon.

A reputable bank will use a multi-stage login system over a secure connection.

MOUSE INPUT Some banks also seek to confound password stealers by using graphical login systems: instead of typing the requested digits from your passcode, you might click the appropriate numbers from a series. This makes it technically much harder for a thief to capture your login details: they need not only to monitor your typing, but also to record your mouse movements and capture what was displayed on the screen in the places you clicked. Note, however, that this doesn't mean it's impossible: there's a class of Trojans called "screen sniffers" that does just this.

DEVICE VALIDATION It's unlikely that a thief trying to access your bank account will be doing so from your own PC. Admittedly, it's not impossible – laptops get stolen, for example. But much online fraud is carried out remotely. This means it can be stopped in its tracks by only allowing users to log on from computers they've confirmed they own. One way of doing this is to challenge the user to answer a greatly extended series of personal questions the first time they log in from an unrecognised device, to provide extra assurance it's really them.

MOBILE SECURITY CODES Another simple way for a bank to confirm that the person logging in is the real account holder is to check whether that person has access to the account-holder's mobile phone. To do this, the bank can send an SMS text message to the account-holder's registered phone number, containing a short security code. The user is then required to enter this code to log in to the banking website. The process is a small inconvenience to the real account-holder, but it should stop an impostor in his tracks. Some banks will also send SMS alerts to customers to confirm unusual actions, such as creating a new payee or transferring an unusual amount of money out of an account. (Indeed, as we noted on p38, banks aren't the only online services to use text messages in this way.)

A variation on the security code theme is to issue bank customers with security tokens – small electronic devices which generate secure codes on demand. If the person trying to log in can provide a valid code, that means he or she has possession of

Some banks require you to use your mobile phone to confirm online transactions.

If your web browser offers to save your banking details, it's a good idea to say no – just in case someone gains access to your PC, or even steals it. We'll talk more about these eventualities on p52-53 and in chapter 10.

the physical token, implying that they're the *bona fide* account-holder. However, tokens cost money to produce and distribute and they're easy to lose, so mobile security codes are more popular.

Even if someone tricks you into revealing your credentials, they still can't access your account

TAN AUTHENTICATION TAN authentication isn't widely used in the UK, but it's a simple and effective system. The bank sends each customer a list of computer-generated codes, known as Transaction Authentication Numbers, and when an account-holder wants to authorise a payment, they enter a TAN to confirm it. If a criminal should manage to steal someone's login credentials and access their account, they can't do any harm without this list of TANs. Each TAN can only be used once, and if the list gets stolen, it can simply be cancelled.

SITEKEY As we discussed on p31, the SiteKey system isn't intended to identify you to your bank: rather, it's designed to prove to you that you're using a real banking service, and not a fake phishing site. It works by showing you a particular picture and phrase chosen by you when you log in – information a scam site wouldn't have access to. SiteKey has one big limitation, however: it's a passive system that relies on you remembering to check for it. If you don't have your wits about you, you might not notice its absence.

GOING BARGAIN HUNTING ON THE INTERNET? HERE ARE SOME POINTERS THAT CAN HELP YOU AVOID FRAUDULENT OR UNTRUSTWORTHY SITES.

Staying safe while shopping online

SHOPPING ONLINE IS EASY – and it can be very cost effective too, thanks to services like Google Shopping that help you find the cheapest price on the net. But cut-price websites can't always be trusted. It's easy for scammers to set up a site, take a few hundred orders, and then shut up shop and vanish. Small legitimate sites are also liable to go abruptly out of business, leaving you out of pocket. Here are some tips for minimising the risks of shopping online.

DOES IT LOOK TRUSTWORTHY? Scammers and fly-by-night site operators don't tend to pay for professional web designers. A site that looks slick and works well suggests there's real investment behind an online store. This alone isn't a guarantee of safety, and scrappy sites aren't always dangerous: sometimes the vendor is simply cutting corners to keep prices low. But a professional-looking site is an encouraging sign.

CHECK FOR CERTIFICATES A secure connection and a verified site identity are good initial indicators of a trustworthy site. If either is missing, be suspicious. See p50 for more details on security certificates.

LOOK FOR ONLINE REVIEWS Odds are, you're not the first person to consider buying from a given website. Before placing your order, try a web search for other people's reviews and experiences: did they get what they paid for? Were they happy with the service?

CONTACT DETAILS A legitimate business should offer a postal address and at least one phone number. If you don't see these, be suspicious – what are you expected to do if there's a problem with your order?

CHECK POLICIES Every online store should publish a privacy policy, detailing how it stores and shares your details. Check the terms are acceptable to you. Again, if there is no policy then the site may be fake, or at best poorly managed. Separately, also check delivery and returns policies, to make sure you don't get stung by unfavourable terms and conditions.

KEEP COPIES OF EVERYTHING If you do place an order, print out the confirmation page and store any emails you receive. These could prove invaluable should you need to raise a dispute or claim a refund.

EXPERT TIP ▼

For high street shopping it's safer to pay for goods with a credit card rather than a debit card, as extra consumer protections apply. Online, however, you get the same protections regardless of the type of card you use. The situation is different with services such as PayPal, however, as we discuss opposite.

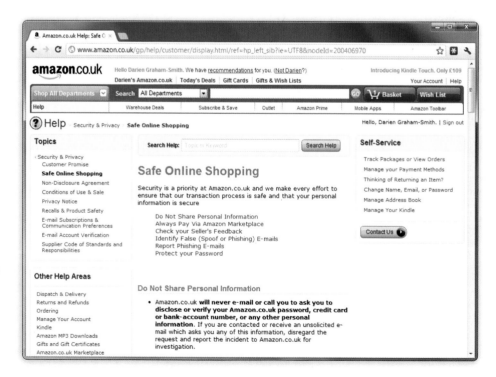

Shopping online can be convenient and safe, so long as you know what risks to look out for.

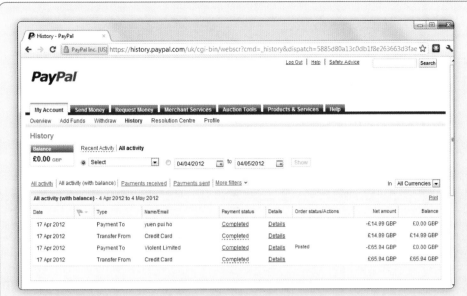

There are plenty of reasons to use PayPal for online transactions – but also some good reasons to be wary.

Another caveat to bear in mind about PayPal is that if you use it to make a card payment (rather than a bank transfer) you'll have to pay a transaction fee – even if you're using a debit card. There are fees for receiving payments too.

PAYPAL PROS AND CONS

In addition to credit and debit cards, many online retailers accept payment via PayPal. If you've used eBay you'll already know PayPal, as it's the default payment option there.

If you're not familiar with PayPal, it's a service that handles money transactions for you. When you want to pay for something online – or send money to a friend or family member – all you have to do is log in to your account at www.paypal.com, enter the recipient's PayPal account name (typically their email address) and authorise the transfer. The funds can come from your bank account, or from a registered credit or debit card. Alternatively, you can send money that other people have previously transferred to your PayPal account.

✔ **QUICK AND EASY** PayPal advertises itself as "the safer, easier way to pay online". And indeed, once you've got an account set up, it's easier to use PayPal than to type in a long credit card number every time you want to buy something. Using PayPal also makes life easier for small online sellers, as it enables them to accept payments without having to open expensive merchant banking accounts and deal with the hassle of card authorisations.

✔ **NO SHARED DETAILS** The "safer" part of PayPal's claim rests on the fact that the person you're sending the money to never has to see your bank details, or your credit card details. This means there's no chance of these details being abused by an unscrupulous merchant – nor

any chance of their being stolen by a hacker who breaks into the merchant's database. If you're unsure about whether to give a website your bank details, PayPal can act as a trusted middleman.

✗ **LIGHTWEIGHT LOGIN SECURITY** On the previous pages we described some of the many measures banks take to ensure your online account can't be compromised. PayPal doesn't have any such protections: to log in and make payments you merely need to provide a standard username and password. This is quick and easy, but it also makes PayPal much more vulnerable to phishing and password stealing attacks than a real bank account. If someone does get into your account, the best thing to do is to change your password, then contact PayPal immediately and report the fraud. But there's no guarantee what will happen next, because...

✗ **NO LEGAL PROTECTION** PayPal isn't a bank, so if something goes wrong with a transaction the familiar consumer protection laws won't apply. PayPal promises to work with its customers to resolve disputed transactions, but there are strict limitations on what you can claim and when; and ultimately PayPal itself is the final arbiter of what gets refunded and what doesn't. PayPal also reserves the right to freeze or seize funds in cases where it considers an account has been used in an inappropriate or suspicious way. Again, if this happens to you, you've very little legal recourse, so we don't recommend using PayPal for large or business-critical transactions.

4
Banking and Shopping

Understanding security certificates

ANYONE CAN CREATE a website. That's a great thing, but it also means that when you're shopping online you can't necessarily tell whether you're dealing with an established retailer or a disreputable chancer. Some websites therefore choose to provide electronic security certificates to establish their good faith – and to enable you to communicate with them over a secure, encrypted connection.

WHAT IS A CERTIFICATE? Simply put, a certificate is a very long number containing coded information about a business or website. Certificates are created by trusted "certificate authorities" (typically large, well-respected companies such as Verisign or Symantec) using a cryptographic process which is readable by all web browsers, but effectively impossible to forge. Site operators can buy certificates for their own sites from certificate authorities – as long as the authority can confirm for itself that the website represents a genuine business.

The presence of a security certificate therefore confirms that you're on a site whose legitimacy has been verified – and not, for example, a phishing site.

Certificates have a second use too: they can be used as cryptographic keys for secure communications, so you can submit confidential information such as credit card details to the site without having to worry they might be intercepted.

TYPES OF CERTIFICATE If the site you're visiting has an "Extended Validation" (EV) certificate – the type that requires the most extensive investigation before it will be issued – you'll see the name of the site owner confirmed in a green box in your browser next to the web address. You can click on this to see more details about the site and the certificate authority.

If the site only has a regular certificate, you won't see the green box. This doesn't necessarily mean the site is fake or insecure, however – it may be that the owner simply didn't feel the need to pay for anything more fancy. So long as you see a padlock icon in your browser (typically in the web address box) and an address that starts with HTTPS, you can be confident that the site has been certified by a recognised authority, and that your browser has established a secure connection.

EXPERT TIP ▼

If your browser keeps complaining about sites providing invalid certificates, check your system clock. Certificates are only valid for a certain period of time: if your date is set wrongly, your browser may think the certificates it receives are out of date, or not yet valid.

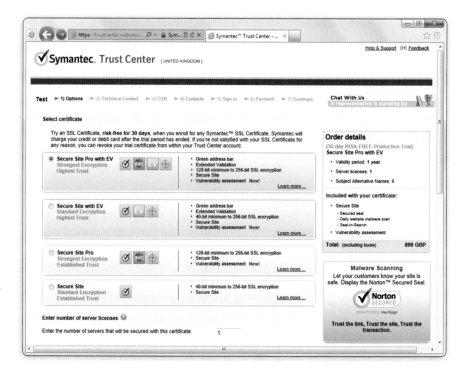

Websites wanting to prove their legitimacy can pay to have a security certificate issued by a trusted third party.

HOW TO...
SHOP SAFELY ON EBAY

1 ▶ CHECK FEEDBACK SCORES

This may seem an obvious tip, but it's worth spelling out. On eBay you're mostly buying from individuals rather than companies, so the issue of trust becomes even more important. That's why every eBay user has a feedback score reflecting how many successful sales they've taken part in. This is shown as a number after their name, along a coloured star. Click on the number and you can see comments that other buyers and sellers have left for that person. Be wary of buying high-value items from people with little feedback, or a mixture of positive and negative comments.

2 ▶ CHECK POSTAGE COSTS

Always check postage costs, especially if you see a desirable item being offered at a surprisingly low price. Some sellers charge extortionate rates for postage, enabling them to advertise lower headline prices – and reducing the fees they have to pay to eBay (since sellers fees are based on purchase price excluding postage). If you don't check the postage before you commit to buying an item, you could be facing a much higher total cost than you realise.

3 ▶ IF IT LOOKS SUPICIOUS...

Checking feedback can help you avoid bad sellers. But eBay users aren't immune to phishing and password-stealing attacks: even the most trustworthy-looking account could conceivably have been hijacked by a scammer hoping to collect some fraudulent payments. So maintain a healthy skepticism, especially if a listing looks suspicious – such as an expensive item with a very low Buy It Now price. Check whether the item and description are consistent with what the seller has offered in the past, and do what you can to confirm the offer is for real (and that the item really exists) before bidding or buying.

4 ▶ BEWARE OF FAKES

In many eBay categories you'll find large quantities of designer products at knock-down prices, typically shipped from the Far East. These items are, without exception, fakes – from imitation Louis Vuitton handbags to dodgy flash memory cards. Not only are these products likely to be of very poor quality, you could be committing a crime in buying one, as there are laws against importing counterfeit goods.

> (!) Sometimes an eBay seller might invite you to complete a sale outside of eBay, ostensibly "to avoid fees". Don't do it! You'll have no comeback whatsoever if the seller simply takes your money and vanishes.

4
Banking and Shopping

HOW LONG?
Teaching LastPass all your passwords and preferences can take a while, but you only have to do it once.

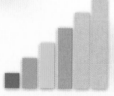

HOW HARD?
Once you've got the hang of LastPass' features, it's very easy to get on with; but there's a definite learning curve while you're getting started.

HOW TO...
SET UP LASTPASS

LastPass is a free program that remembers login details for all your online accounts, and saves you time filling in forms too

1▶ DOWNLOAD AND INSTALL
Visit www.lastpass.com – noting that the site's identity is confirmed by a green EV certificate (see p50) – and click to download the free LastPass software. If you find LastPass useful, you might later choose to upgrade to the Premium edition, but let's take the free service for a test-drive first. Click the download link, save the file to your hard disk and run the installer.

2▶ CHOOSE A BROWSER AND CREATE A NEW ACCOUNT
The installer adds a plug-in to your web browser. First pick which browser(s) you want to use: you'll need to close it while the plug-in is installed. Next, you'll be prompted to create a LastPass account, where your passwords will be stored. Accept the default option: if you later install LastPass on a second PC, choose "I already have an account" and your details will be imported to that PC.

3▶ ENTER YOUR DETAILS
You'll now be asked to provide a few account details. The password you choose will be the gateway to *all* of your secure accounts, so make sure it's secure and memorable (see p42 for some tips). Create a reminder for yourself too. Then, tick the boxes below to accept the terms and conditions and click Next. You'll be prompted to re-enter your LastPass password, just to make absolutely certain you typed it correctly.

4▶ IMPORT INSECURE DATA
The installer will now offer to scan for insecure data, to find any passwords saved on your system by web browsers. By default, LastPass will learn all of these passwords: if there are any passwords you don't want imported, deselect them by clicking the padlock at the right of the column. You can view stored passwords by ticking the "Reveal Passwords?" box. Click Next to continue.

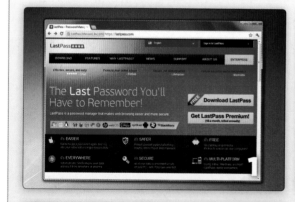

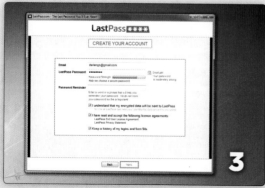

5 ▶ REMOVE INSECURE DATA

It won't have escaped your notice that if LastPass can extract saved login and password details from your system, a Trojan could do so too: In the next window accept "remove all items that were imported into LastPass" to wipe these vulnerable details from your system. LastPass stores passwords in an encrypted format, so your credentials are safe.

This is the last step of setup: click Next and then Done to proceed. You then have the option of watching a short video tutorial: this is an easy way to get a quick overview of what LastPass can do.

6 ▶ START USING LASTPASS

The next time you open your browser you'll see a new "asterisk" icon for LastPass. Click this to enter your password and start using LastPass. From now on, whenever you visit a site and enter a password, LastPass will offer to remember it securely for you, and can log you in automatically whenever you return. Click again on the LastPass icon to see a drop-down menu of various tools and options.

7 ▶ AUTOMATIC FORM FILLING

When you right-click your mouse you'll see a new contextual menu has appeared for LastPass. This offers several features, including the ability to fill in online forms automatically – so you never need to type out your address and credit card details by hand ever again. To get started, select **LastPass ▶ Fill Forms ▶ Add Profile** from the menu. Type in whichever details you want to store and give your new profile a name. The next time you visit a site that asks for these details, select the appropriate profile from the right-click menu and your details will be magically filled in.

8 ▶ GENERATE SECURE PASSWORDS

It's all very well having LastPass remember your credentials for you, but if you're using low-quality passwords like "123456" your account could still be hacked. Next time you change your password, right-click and select **LastPass ▶ Generate Password** to produce a secure, unguessable string of letters and numbers. You may not be able to remember it, but that doesn't matter – LastPass will remember it for you!

EXPERT TIP ▼

If you leave your computer unattended while you're logged into LastPass, someone else could come along and gain access to all of your online accounts. But you can easily configure LastPass to automatically log you out after a certain period of inactivity: to set this option, click on the LastPass icon and select Preferences.

IN THIS CHAPTER

Chapter

5

NETWORKING

Computers are more capable, more convenient and more fun when they're connected together. From little home networks to the big wide internet, networking is everywhere these days. Unfortunately, if computers can talk to one another, they can also infect one another. In this chapter we examine the

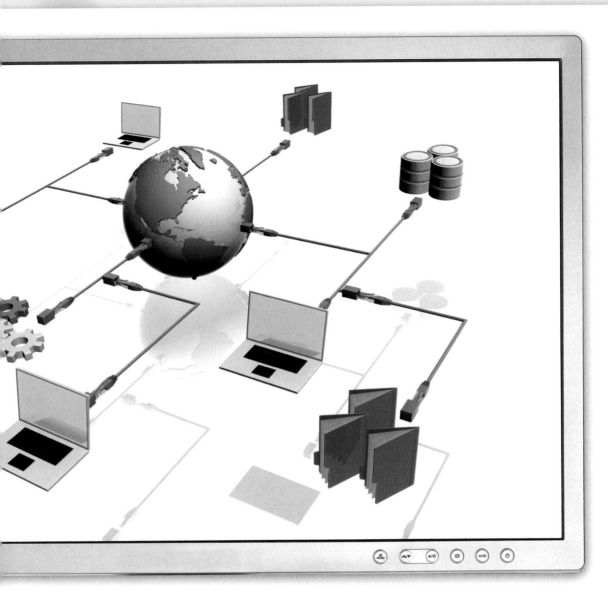

DANGERS

dangerous breed of network-borne malware known as "worms", and peer into the shadowy world of "botnets". We also show you how to secure your home network against intruders, and how to ensure your personal information isn't shared with the world at large when you use a public Wi-Fi hotspot.

▶ IF YOUR COMPUTER'S CONNECTED TO A NETWORK, IT COULD BE VULNERABLE TO A WORM – PERHAPS THE MOST SNEAKY SORT OF MALWARE THERE IS.

What is a network worm?

IN CHAPTER 1 WE DESCRIBED two common types of malware, namely viruses and Trojans. A worm is a third type of malware. It works similarly to a virus – indeed, some experts consider that worms are a subspecies of virus. But worms work in a very particular way. Whereas a virus spreads by infecting a floppy disk, or an executable file, a worm spreads by copying itself directly from computer to computer over a network. This makes worms the most insidious type of malware there is. If there's a worm at large on your network, you don't need to run a program, visit a website or do anything whatsoever to be infected: the worm will find its way onto your system automatically.

HOW WORMS SPREAD All worms spread by replicating themselves across a network, but different worms use different approaches. Arguably, the email-borne viruses we described in Chapter 1 can be counted as worms, because they spread from computer to computer via the email network.

Another approach is for a worm to silently copy itself onto each Windows PC it can find. The worm then remotely updates the Registry (where

Windows stores information such as system settings) so that the file is run automatically at start up, causing the system to become infected whenever it's next rebooted. An infection like this can be a big problem for a home or business network, because the worm must be removed from every PC at once. Otherwise, as soon as each PC is cleaned, it will be re-infected by one of the other machines.

Home and business networks, however, are only the tip of the iceberg. The biggest danger is from worms that are designed to spread over the internet, as these have the potential to infect literally billions of devices all around the world.

HOW WORMS GET IN In theory it ought to be impossible for a program to connect to your PC and install itself automatically over the internet. It's something operating system developers actively try to prevent, for obvious reasons.

The authors of internet worms therefore have to employ tactics similar to those used in creating a drive-by download (see p9). They rely on finding vulnerabilities in the operating system – "exploits",

EXPERT TIP ▾

When you buy a new PC or laptop, it's likely to be many months or even years behind the latest security patches. Make sure you run Windows Update at your earliest convenience – until you do, you're a sitting duck for worms. You might need to restart your PC and re-run Windows Update a few times to get completely up to date.

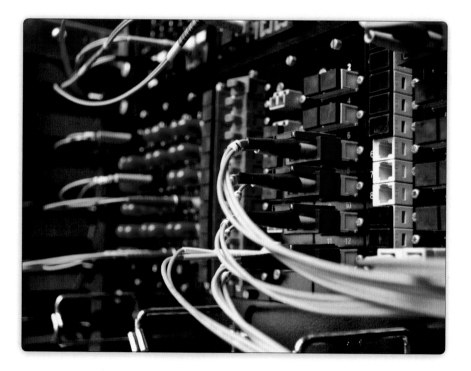

An internet worm can infect billions of computers in a matter of minutes.

as they're called – to gain access. Some worms have the ability to make use of more than one exploit, so if one vulnerability has already been patched, the worm may still be able to get in via a different route. In a few cases, worms have also been capable of virus-like behaviour, allowing them to spread across both networks and removable USB drives. The cleverest worms can even periodically "phone home" for updates. In this way, the malware creator can keep updating the code to work with new exploits and replication methods.

This side of things may sound quite sophisticated, but the actual operation of a worm is mindless and indiscriminate. Typically a worm will sit on your PC and try to connect to internet addresses at random until it finds one that's susceptible to a recognised exploit. Then, it will make use of the exploit to install a copy of the worm code on the remote PC – before going back to scanning randomly for more potential hosts.

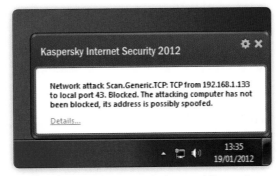

The threat from network attacks is every bit as serious as the dangers of regular malware.

started up a workstation that was infected with Blaster, the computer would automatically shut down again almost immediately, making the computer effectively unusable.

Clearly that's a frustrating and disruptive state of affairs. Arguably, however, a bigger concern is worms that keep a low profile, so you don't realise you're infected. After all, a worm running on your PC can do anything a regular Trojan can, including monitoring your keyboard to steal passwords. Worms

If you work in an office where people regularly connect their own laptops to the company network, be warned – there's a distinct danger that someone could bring an infection in from outside and spread it around the office.

THE DANGERS OF WORMS

There are several reasons why it's undesirable to have a worm running on your network. The first is a simple matter of resources. If there are five, or ten, or a hundred computers on your local network all constantly scanning for addresses to infect, that adds up to a lot of traffic. It may be enough to overwhelm your router or other network hardware, causing everyone to lose access to the network entirely. This is similar in principle to a Denial of Service attack – see p60. But in this case it's not done deliberately, but as a collateral effect of worms simply doing their job.

UNKNOWN SOFTWARE

Even if your network can easily cope with the worm traffic, it's always undesirable to have unknown code running on your PC, especially code that's clearly been created by someone unscrupulous. After all, while a worm's defining function is spreading across a network, there's no guarantee that it won't carry a malicious component as well – what's called a "payload" in security jargon.

One memorably malicious worm was the notorious Blaster worm, believed to have infected more than 8 million PCs back in 2003. When you

The authors of worms employ tactics similar to those used in creating a drive-by download

can also subsume your system into what's called a "botnet", a network of computers that can be controlled from afar. See p60 for more on botnets.

PROTECTION AGAINST WORMS

Many worms rely on unpatched exploits to spread. If you run Windows Update regularly and install security updates as they become available, you'll greatly reduce your chances of being infected by a worm. It's hard to overstate the importance of keeping up to date: in 2008 a worm called Conficker infected an estimated 15 million PCs worldwide – using a vulnerability which had already been fixed via Windows Update.

Installing updates isn't the only way to stay safe. Worms are programs that must install and run on your PC to be effective; and so, just like viruses and Trojans, they can be detected and removed by antivirus software. An even better approach is to prevent them from reaching your computer in the first place. On the following pages we'll show you how a firewall can do just that.

▶ YOUR COMPUTER DOESN'T HAVE TO BE AN OPEN TARGET. A FIREWALL CAN DEFEND AGAINST WORMS AND OTHER ATTACKS BY PREVENTING UNWANTED CONNECTIONS.

Blocking attacks with a firewall

AS WE MENTIONED on the previous pages, worms are a particularly nasty threat because you don't have to do anything at all to get infected – you just have to be on the same network as an infected PC. In princple, therefore, the best way to defend yourself against worms is to keep your computer disconnected from networks of any type. Clearly, this isn't realistic for most of us; but using a firewall it's possible to get a similar effect by blocking unwanted network traffic.

WHAT IS A FIREWALL? A firewall is ordinarily a piece of software that runs on your computer and hooks into Windows' networking system. It acts as a sort of supervisor for network connections: whenever a remote computer tries to communicate with your PC, the firewall decides whether to allow it or whether to block the connection. The name derives from a construction term, meaning a wall that is literally built to withstand a fire. However, whereas a physical firewall is an impenetrable barrier, computer firewalls can be finely configured, allowing you to perform whatever network tasks you wish, while unauthorised operations are excluded.

WHERE DO I GET A FIREWALL? The odds are you already have a firewall, though you may not realise it. After numerous embarrassing worm attacks in the early 2000s, Microsoft added a firewall component to Windows, so all editions of the operating system after Windows XP Service Pack 2 have this protection built in. You may not have realised this firewall is protecting you, however, as it's designed not to interfere with typical online activities such as browsing the web and sharing files – and when it does detect a worm trying to connect to your PC, the connection is silently blocked.

No software system is perfect, however: malware authors are constantly looking for exploits that will allow them to sneak under the radar. Despite the ubiquity of the Windows Firewall in recent years, high-profile attacks such as the Storm worm (2007) and the Conficker worm (2008) have still managed to infect tens of millions of PCs.

This is one reason why you might choose to use a third-party firewall instead. These are typically included in commercial security suites, as we discuss in Chapter 8. Though a non-Microsoft firewall may

EXPERT TIP ▼

Many businesses use hardware firewall appliances that let them allow or block specific types of connection across the whole company. Your domestic router may have firewall features too, in addition to the protections we describe on p61; but for an individual, a software firewall is perfectly sufficient to keep you safe, and it's normally easier to use.

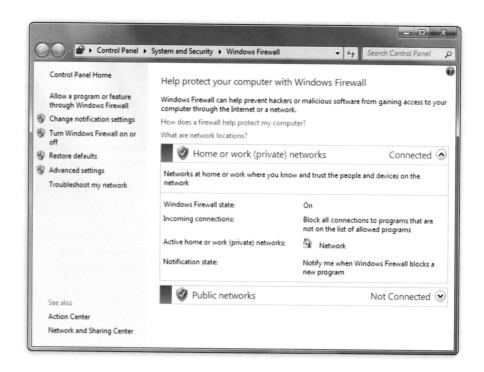

The Windows Firewall quietly keeps you safe from many network-borne dangers.

Advanced firewall settings let you specify which programs may communicate on which ports.

not be any more watertight, it probably won't share the same vulnerabilities, making it less susceptible to mass infections.

Third-party firewalls often provide more technical detail of what's happening on your network, and give you more control over which connections are permitted and which are blocked – in contrast to the Windows Firewall, which prefers to keep as quiet as possible. For more on third-party firewalls, see p92.

TWO-WAY FILTERING It's essential for a firewall to monitor incoming network connections. But many firewalls also monitor and manage the outbound connections made by programs installed on your PC. This is sensible for a few reasons. First, if a new program appears unexpectedly on your system and starts trying make network connections, you want to know about it: this is malware-like behaviour, and could indicate that you've contracted an infection that needs removing.

Second, by blocking these connections (unless you explicitly authorise them), the firewall can prevent a worm from infecting other systems on your network – forestalling a major epidemic. Most third-party firewalls are full two-way systems, but the Windows Firewall only has limited capabilities when it comes to monitoring installed programs. It will warn you when a program invites incoming connections, but it won't actively scan outbound connections.

PORTS We've spoken so far in general terms about network connections. In order to understand a little better how a firewall differentiates between authorised and unauthorised connections, it's necessary to talk a little about ports.

Whenever one computer tries to open a connection to another, it must specify a "port" to connect to. These ports are purely notional: in reality, of course, all network traffic goes via the same route – either through an Ethernet cable or over a Wi-Fi link. But from the computer's perspective, each port is a discrete interface, which is handled by a particular network service. For example, port 445 is used by Windows' file-sharing system, while port 80 is ordinarily used by web server software.

This makes it easy for a single computer to host multiple network services without conflicts. Remote systems can specify what sort of connection they want to open simply by directing their connection to the appropriate port. There's no particular logic behind which port number relates to which service – it's just a conventional system, which is managed

After embarrassing worm attacks in the early 2000s, Microsoft added a firewall to Windows

and maintained by a body called the IANA (Internet Assigned Numbers Authority).

With this information, we can understand more easily how worms are able to exploit vulnerabilities in Windows. Let's imagine a weakness is discovered in the Windows Remote Desktop system. A worm might well target this weakness by connecting to the port used by Remote Desktop (which happens to be number 3389) and sending malicious data directly to it.

If a firewall is installed on the system, however, a worm won't be able to get through. The Windows Firewall blocks all connection attempts on port 3389 by default – you have to deliberately open it if you want to use Remote Desktop. Third-party firewalls will normally detect the connection and ask you if you're expecting a connection of this type, from this particular internet address. If you're not, you can simply block the connection at the click of a mouse. Meanwhile, communications on other ports – such as Windows file-sharing connections on port 445 – can continue unhindered.

> ! Firewalls can interfere with legitimate programs, such as games and network tools. If something isn't working as it should, you can try temporarily disabling your firewall to see if that's the cause. Don't leave it switched off though!

What is a "botnet"?

"Bots" are computers that have had malicious "back door" remote control software installed, so they can be controlled over the internet by a third party. A botnet is a network of compromised PCs which are all under the control of the same person or organisation. In recent years, various worms and Trojans have managed to subsume tens of millions of PCs into botnets. This is bad news – and not just for the people whose computers are infected.

THE DANGERS TO YOU If your computer becomes part of a botnet, the person controlling the botnet will have gained the power to install and run whatever software they like on your PC, without your permission or knowledge. Your personal information and the security and stability of your PC will be completely at their mercy. And at any point the operator could "pull the plug" and trash your system entirely. It's a sobering thought – and, what's more, being part of a botnet also means your PC is likely to be used in criminal acts against others.

THE DANGERS TO OTHERS A botnet can be used for many illegal and antisocial purposes. If a malware creator comes up with a new worm or virus, seeding it through a botnet of millions of PCs is an extremely

effective way to propagate it into the wild. Botnets are also an effective way to distribute spam: it's hard for email services to detect and block junk mail when it's coming from a million different senders.

A botnet can alternatively be used as a weapon against an online service: in a "Distributed Denial of Service" attack, a huge number of computers send simultaneous connection requests to the target system, overwhelming it and making it unresponsive. It's also been suggested that the combined power of all the systems in the botnet could be used to try to crack passwords or break into systems by brute force.

Clearly a botnet is a very powerful thing, and many operators make money by hiring their botnets out to other criminals. A botnet may thus be used for one crime one week and a quite different one the next.

VULNERABILITIES A good antivirus package should detect and remove botnet software from your PC. But not everyone can be relied on to keep their PC clean. The only certain way to put a stop to a botnet's evil deeds is to compromise its control mechanism. Security professionals may try to do this by taking control of the internet address from which instructions are issued, then sending instructions that order the botnet to delete itself.

CAN A ROUTER PROTECT YOU?

A router may not provide perfect protection, but it's unquestionably safer than connecting a computer directly to the internet via a cable or ADSL modem. For safety and convenience we strongly recommend you use a router.

You may have heard that if you use a router (which almost all of us do these days) then you're protected from network attacks. There is some truth in this, but it isn't the whole story. It's worth understanding the ways in which a router can protect you – and the ways in which it can't.

✓ **SHARED IPV4 ADDRESS** We mentioned on p57 that some worms spread by trying to connect to random internet addresses. The good news is, if you have a typical domestic router setup, you're immune to attacks like this – at least, ones that use the IPv4 addressing system, which is the most common one worldwide. No matter how many computers you may own, your household has just a single "external" IPv4 address (that is, one accessible from outside of your home). And that address belongs to your router. In ordinary use, the router allows computers on your network to make outgoing connections through this address, and forwards responses back to the originating systems. But if an incoming connection arrives out of the blue, the router won't know which computer it's intended for, and will drop the connection, leaving your PCs unmolested.

✗ **THE SWITCH TO IPV6** As we mentioned above, IPv4 is the most widely used internet addressing system. However, it's gradually being replaced by the more advanced IPv6 system, with ISPs and router manufacturers increasingly using the two systems in parallel. With IPv6, each computer on your home network gets its own external address, which can be targeted directly by a worm. The protection we describe above simply doesn't apply.

✓ **NO EXPOSED PORTS** It's not all bad news. Even if a remote server does manage to connect to your PC, most exploits require access to a specific port. By default, routers typically come set to allow traffic on a handful of preconfigured ports, greatly limiting the scope for an attacker to exploit remote vulnerabilities.

✗ **THE RISK OF UPNP** Having ports closed off by default can prevent some types of attack; but it can also interfere with legitimate software, such as games and network tools. To compensate for this, most routers support a system called UPnP – short for "Universal Plug 'n' Play". This lets programs running on your PC configure the router settings they need automatically, so that everything works without your having to lift a finger. The attraction of UPnP is obvious, but there's a danger too: if a legitimate program can use UPnP to open up ports, it's possible for malware to do the same. For this reason, UPnP is normally switched off by default in router settings. If you choose to enable it, be warned that you're making yourself slightly more vulnerable to worms and similar threats.

HOW TO...
SECURE YOUR ROUTER

If intruders can access your home network, they could browse your files or infect you with malware. Here's how to keep them out.

1 ▶ POSITION YOUR ROUTER SECURELY
Keeping your home network safe means ensuring no unauthorised users can connect. A practical first step is to ensure your Wi-Fi signal isn't "leaking" into neighbouring homes, or out into the street, any more than is unavoidable. Consider moving your router towards the rear of your house, or going into its settings and turning down the transmission power. The idea is to minimise the number of spots outside your home from which it's possible to connect.

2 ▶ UPGRADE YOUR ROUTER FIRMWARE
It's very rare that routers are found to have serious a security vulnerabilities, but – as with Windows – it's always a good idea to check for firmware updates, just in case there is a patch to apply. You'll normally find this option in your router configuration pages. A firmware update may also bring other useful features or improve stability.

3 ▶ SET AN ADMINISTRATOR PASSWORD
A great many router models use the same default user name and password to protect their configuration pages. This is common knowledge, especially among hackers. Make sure you change these credentials – otherwise anyone who gets onto your network will be able to reconfigure your router to allow whatever activity they wish.

4 ▶ CHANGE YOUR SSID
The SSID is the name of your wireless network (it stands, prosaically, for Service Set Identifier). Most routers come with a generic SSID, typically the manufacturer's name. If a network administrator hasn't changed this name, that suggests that other settings may have been left at their defaults too – a prospect which may encourage would-be intruders. It's best to change the SSID – plus, it avoids confusion when your neighbour buys a router from the same manufacturer.

HOW LONG?
You can spend hours tinkering with router settings, but these eight steps won't take too long.

HOW HARD?
It's easy to be put off by the rather Byzantine configuration interfaces of some routers, but these are basic settings that should be easy to find.

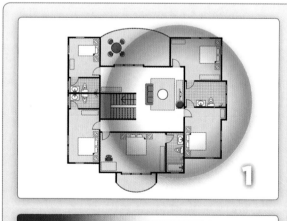

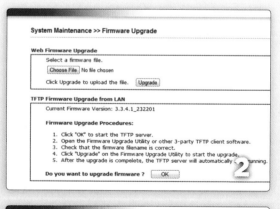

System Maintenance >> Firmware Upgrade

Web Firmware Upgrade
Select a firmware file.
Choose File No file chosen
Click Upgrade to upload the file.　Upgrade

TFTP Firmware Upgrade from LAN
Current Firmware Version: 3.3.4.1_232201

Firmware Upgrade Procedures:
1. Click "OK" to start the TFTP server.
2. Open the Firmware Upgrade Utility or other 3-party TFTP client software.
3. Check that the firmware filename is correct.
4. Click "Upgrade" on the Firmware Upgrade Utility to start the upgrade.
5. After the upgrade is complete, the TFTP server will automatically ... running.

Do you want to upgrade firmware ?　OK

System Maintenance >> Administrator Password Setup

Administrator Password

Old Password	••••••••••
New Password	
Confirm Password	

OK

Wireless LAN >> General Setup

General Setting (IEEE 802.11)
☑ Enable Wireless LAN
Mode :　Mixed(11b+11g+11n) ▾

Index(1-15) in Schedule Setup: ___, ___, ___, ___
Only schedule profiles that have the action "Force Down" are applied to the WLAN, all other actions are ignored.

	Enable	Hide SSID	SSID	Isolate Member	Isolate VP
1		☑	Supanet		
2	☑	☐		☐	☐
3	☑	☐		☐	☐
4	☑	☐		☐	☐

Isolate Member: Wireless clients (stations) with the same SSID cannot access for ea... other.

5 ▶ USE STRONG ENCRYPTION

It goes without saying that you should use a secure password (sometimes called passkey) on your wireless network. But it's also important to choose the right encryption technology. Many routers still support an old standard called WEP (Wired Equivalent Privacy), but with modern tools it's possible for a hacker to break into a WEP-protected wireless network in minutes. Use WPA2 (sometimes called WPA2-PSK) instead: it works in the same way as WEP but is effectively unbreakable.

6 ▶ USE MAC ADDRESS FILTERING

Every device that connects to your router has a unique Media Access Control (MAC) address. This address is programmed into the hardware, so it should never change. If you enable MAC address filtering on your router, you can specify a "whitelist" of MAC addresses that are allowed to connect to your home network. Anybody with an unauthorised device will then be unable to connect even if they have the right passkey. This provides a high level of security – but it can be a pain having to authorise every new device that comes into your home.

7 ▶ LOCK DOWN ADMINISTRATION

On many routers you can disable wireless administration, so only computers that are physically connected to the router via an Ethernet cable are permitted to change configuration settings. The benefit of this is self-evident – it makes it impossible for someone to stand outside your window with an iPhone and mess with your security settings. However, if you don't have a desktop computer that's regularly connected to the router by a cable, then, like MAC address filtering, you may consider this measure more hassle than it's worth.

8 ▶ DISABLE UPNP

As we described on p61, UPnP – or "Universal Plug 'n' Play", to give it its full title – is a convenient system that allows programs running on your PC to make changes to your router configuration. In theory, though, it could be a security risk: for example, a Trojan might abuse UPnP to reduce your security settings, making it easier for a worm to infect your PC. If you can live without it, disabling UPnP is a sensible way to give your home security a boost.

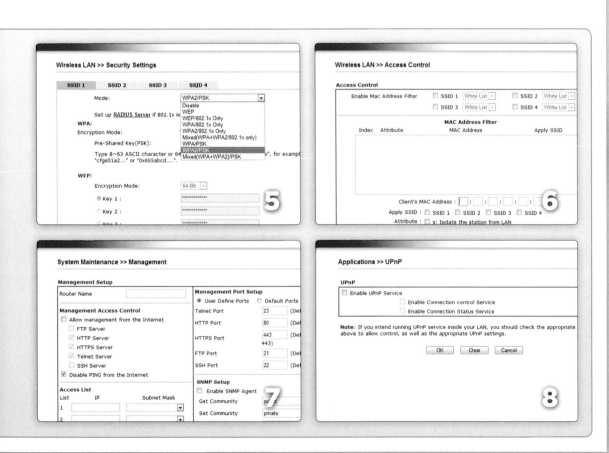

EXPERT TIP ▼

If you're not sure how to access the settings for your router, check the manual, or look online. Remember that different brands and models of router have different interfaces, so once you're in, your options may not look like the examples here; they may not even use precisely the same terms. Don't panic – this is just a quirk of the router industry.

HOW TO...
STAY STAFE IN A HOTSPOT

Wi-Fi hotspots make it possible to work wherever you go – but it's important to know the risks associated with public networks.

1▶ CONNECT VIA A SECURE NETWORK

Many wireless hotspots are "open", so no password is needed to connect (though you might need one to connect to the internet). Windows marks open networks with a golden shield icon. Your communications across an open network like this aren't secure at all: anything you transmit could be monitored by any other computer user nearby. If possible, use a secure network with a password. On a network like this, your traffic is completely private, even from other users on the same network.

2▶ BEWARE OF FAKE HOTSPOTS

In public places like airports and hotels, criminals have been known to create fake wireless networks. If you connect, you might be tricked into entering credit card details, or a web page might attempt a drive-by download of malware on your PC. When you see a promising-looking SSID, check it belongs to a genuine hotspot before connecting.

3▶ SET LOCATION TO "PUBLIC"

The first time you connect to a new network, Windows will pop up a requester asking you to choose whether this is a Home, Work or Public network. If you choose a Home or Work network, helpful services such as file and printer sharing will be enabled. Pick Public network and these features are disabled automatically, making it harder for anyone else to access your files, or to get unwanted software onto your machine.

4▶ KEEP TRACK OF FIREWALL SETTINGS

File sharing isn't the only thing that's locked down on a Public network: many strict firewall rules are applied too, which can prevent some programs from working. If you choose, you can tell Windows to relax these rules so you can get your work done in a public place. But be aware: when you do this, the change applies to *all* Public networks you might connect to in future.

HOW LONG?
It should only take a moment to digest these tips, and to put them to work next time you visit a hotspot.

HOW HARD?
If you want to get stuck into configuring firewall and VPN settings, things can get technical. But for the most part, staying safe is common sense.

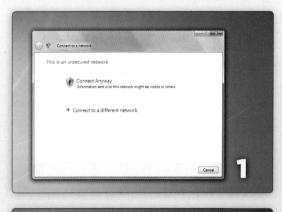

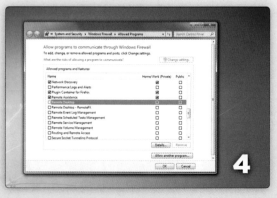

5 ▶ WATCH FOR "SHOULDER SURFERS"

A very low-tech piece of advice, but a crucial one nonetheless. In a public place like a café, there may well be someone standing or sitting behind you while you use your computer. It's possible that this person can see your screen – so be cautious of bringing up any confidential information. It's even possible that someone could watch your keyboard while you log in to a service and see, from your typing, what your password is. A quick glance over the shoulder should tell you whether there's any danger of your credentials being seen. Of course, you can also make it much less likely that a "shoulder surfer" will be able to catch your password if you use a long, unguessable one.

6 ▶ DON'T TRUST UNKNOWN HOTSPOTS

All the security precautions in the world won't keep you safe if someone's hacked the hotspot itself – or if it's being operated by criminals. Unfortunately, there's no way for you to check the trustworthiness of a wireless network, so it's best to avoid unknown hotspots – and be cautious of banking and shopping over Wi-Fi.

7 ▶ CONSIDER USING A VPN

If you're on a business trip, and need to connect to a server back at the office – for example, to pick up your email – then security and privacy are essential. Ask your IT staff whether it's possible to use a VPN (a "virtual private network" to its friends). This is a secure connection that you can create directly between your PC and another system. All traffic that's sent over a VPN is encrypted, so even if you're using a hotspot, you can pick up emails and even access file servers via the VPN without having to worry that your information might be monitored or stolen.

8 ▶ DON'T ASSUME WIRED IS SAFER

In some hotels you'll get the option of either using a wireless connection or plugging in an Ethernet cable. You might expect the cable to be more secure – after all, it's a direct line to the router. But because of the way Ethernet works, it might in fact be possible for anyone else in the hotel to see your network traffic. A cable connection may be faster, but when it comes to privacy a secure wireless connection wins hands down.

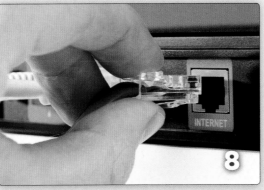

EXPERT TIP ▼

An "evil twin" attack is when a criminal creates a fake wireless network with the same name as a legitimate one – and operates it in the same place. It's a sneaky trick, as there's no way for you to tell which is the real, safe network. All you can do is talk to the hotspot operator and proceed with extreme caution.

Mp3 & Audio
Network Tools
Other
Photo & Design
Security & Antiv
System Utilities
Video
Web Developme
Windows Tools

Popular links:
› Editor Reviews
› Most popular
› New releases
› Our picks
› Essential downlo
› Windows RSS fe

Mac
Mobile

**Safe, Trusted a
Spyware Free**
All software on Soft3
been tested to ensu
100% free of spywa
and other malware.

Chapter

6

SPYWARE AND

Spyware and adware aren't destructive in the same way as regular viruses and Trojans. And in many cases they don't sneak onto your PC through the back door – they're openly included with legitimate downloads. All the same, these types of software can compromise your privacy, hijack your browser

ADWARE

and interfere with your computer usage in any
number of other ways. In this chapter we explain
how spyware works, detail the dangers and give
examples of infamous spyware packages of the
past. And, of course, we advise you on what to do if
you discover spyware is running on your own PC.

SPYWARE IS AN UNUSUAL CATEGORY OF SOFTWARE: IT SPREADS IN DIFFERENT WAYS TO CONVENTIONAL MALWARE, AND SOME PEOPLE ARGUE IT ISN'T MALWARE AT ALL.

What is spyware, and is it malware?

MOST ANTIVIRUS PACKAGES promise to protect you against not only viruses and Trojans but spyware as well – so you'd be forgive for assuming that spyware is another clearly defined type of malware. In reality, there's no clear, universal definition of exactly what constitutes spyware and what doesn't. But there is a loose consensus about the sort of thing we mean when we use the term.

WHAT IS SPYWARE? The term "spyware" suggests any software that spies on you, and some people do use the word to refer to – for example – Trojans that monitor your keyboard to steal passwords. However, antivirus software normally categorises such threats as straightforward malware. Security experts conventionally use "spyware" in a more nuanced way, and this is the usage we'll follow on these pages.

Spyware in this sense is a specific type of spying program: one which monitors which web sites you visit, and sends this information back to advertisers. The advertisers can then use this illicitly gained information to target you with adverts that reflect your interests. To increase the effectiveness of

this ruse, the spyware may also hijack your browser to ensure you see these adverts – perhaps opening them in pop-up windows, inserting them into web pages you visit, or even quietly filtering out existing adverts and replacing them with ones from favoured advertisers.

Rather counterintuitively, the term "spyware" is also sometimes used to refer to any program that places adverts in your browser, or opens them in pop-up windows, even where this software *hasn't* collected any personal information about your browsing habits. This type of software is sometimes referred to as "adware" (though that term can also refer to software that displays adverts within its own interface).

Spyware isn't just about adverts. Some spyware tampers with web searches, giving certain sites a much higher ranking than they really deserve. Spyware may also add a new search toolbar to your browser, to encourage you to use an advertiser's own search engine, which will again naturally promote their favoured sites.

Another scam is injecting affiliate links into web pages. This way, every time someone using the spyware clicks on a link to buy a product from an

Programs that put adverts on your desktop are typically quite up-front about what they do.

online retailer such as Amazon, the spyware author gets a small kickback from the retailer.

Overall, spyware isn't defined by a single clear characteristic; but we can say in general that if something exploits or interferes with your online activities for commercial purposes, it probably qualifies as spyware.

HOW DOES SPYWARE SPREAD? Another big difference between spyware and regular malware is the way each one gets onto your PC. As we've discussed in previous chapters, malware such as viruses, Trojans and worms sneak onto your system via underhand methods – either by exploiting loopholes in your system, or by tricking you into installing something you didn't mean to.

Spyware, on the other hand, often installs in plain sight. Typically, a spyware application might come bundled along with the installer for a legitimate piece of software, but it won't be surreptitiously piggybacking like a Trojan. If you read the details of the installer, you'll normally be made aware that the spyware will be installed by default, and you'll have the opportunity to opt out. If you agree to install the spyware, you may even be asked to agree to a set of terms and conditions which explain what the software does. Once the spyware is installed, it may provide an uninstallation routine – though some spyware makes itself deliberately difficult to remove.

Of course, the authors are hoping you won't realise what the software is, won't bother to read the terms and conditions – and hence won't realise that it's in your best interest to opt out of the installation, or to remove the program at your first opportunity. But the mere fact that the installation takes place in the open is a significant difference between spyware and other types of malware.

IS SPYWARE MALWARE? This gives rise to a tricky question. Is spyware itself a form of malware? The authors would argue it's not, since the user chooses to install the software and is, notionally, informed of what it does. It's not a crime to hijack your own web browser, after all. And to date, no spyware distributor has been prosecuted under the legislation

that normally covers malware infections (that being, in the UK, the Computer Misuse Act 1990).

Yet it's hard to imagine that many people would choose to install spyware on their PC if they knew what it did. It seems much more likely that the vast majority of installations are inadvertent and unwanted, Hence, as we mentioned above, most antivirus packages promise to remove spyware from your PC, effectively treating it as malware.

> *It's hard to imagine many people would install spyware on their PC if they knew what it did*

Since there's no firm definition of spyware, not all antivirus developers agree on which programs qualify for the term. When your antivirus software detects a spyware-like application on your system, you may be asked to make a judgment call yourself as to whether it should be removed. Unless you recognise it as useful, it's normally a good idea to get rid of it.

LICENCE RESTRICTIONS Spyware authors who want their applications to appear respectable will normally allow you to uninstall the software if you choose. However, they may try to discourage this by tying the licence to some piece of actually useful software. If you want to uninstall the spyware you're obliged to remove the useful software too.

If you choose to ignore a licence like this, and just remove the spyware, we very much doubt the spyware distributor will ever find out. But it would be much better to remove both, and switch to software from a genuinely respectable developer – one who doesn't try to blackmail you into running spyware.

The dangers of spyware

NOW WE'VE EXPLAINED what spyware is, and where it comes from, you might think it's not a serious concern. After all, does it really matter if you end up seeing one advert rather than another? Or if someone makes a little money off a purchase you were going to make anyway?

To be sure, the behaviour of spyware and adware appears less alarming than that of password-stealing Trojans – remembering that, in the conventional usage we're following here, such unequivocally malicious nasties aren't counted as spyware. But there are still plenty of reasons to avoid installing spyware on your system, or to remove it as soon as you discover it.

PC PERFORMANCE All software takes up memory and consumes CPU processes while it's running – and spyware is likely to be running all the time, or at least all the time you have a web browser open. It's unlikely that a piece of spyware will be so huge and unwieldy that it single-handedly slows your PC to a crawl; but it may nevertheless make a visible difference to how quickly pages appear in your browser, especially if the

spyware engages in rewriting web pages as they're loaded, to insert the spyware author's own adverts or alter search engine results.

Even if your PC's technical performance isn't perceptibly compromised, spyware can slow you down. For example, if your PC's infected with a spyware program that keeps popping up adverts, you'll have to keep stopping what you're doing to close the windows – an irritating interruption. Spyware that adds a toolbar to your browser also reduces the amount of space available for web pages. On a large desktop monitor that might not be a serious concern, but on a compact laptop or netbook screen you need all the space you can get. There's a reason why the latest versions of all the popular browsers keep their controls as compact as possible, and display only a bare minimum of toolbars by default.

NETWORK PERFORMANCE Spyware running on your PC can add significantly to your network traffic. That's because, for every web page you download, the spyware may also be fetching additional adverts and information from its own servers. If you have a home

Installing browser add-ons has an inevitable impact on your system resources – and can clog up your network connection too.

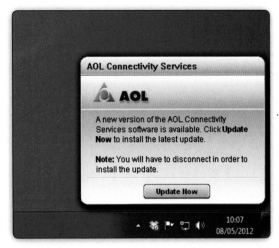

Self-updating spyware means you can never be certain exactly what's happening on your PC (see box, right).

Sometimes an update to a legitimate application will bring new spyware-type features. But equally, applications have been known to clean up their act and stop being spyware – the AOL software pictured to the left being a case in point.

network of several PCs all infected with spyware, the cumulative effect could again be quite noticeable, especially if you have a slow internet connection. For a business, more traffic means more work for the central network hardware to do, more connections to monitor and less bandwidth to go around.

UNKNOWN BEHAVIOUR Spyware is more up-front than other types of malware – as we mentioned on the previous page, it's normally possible to choose not to install it, and it may well come with a licence that explains what it does.

In practice, however, if you have spyware on your system, it's probably because you absent-mindedly clicked through an installer without realising exactly what you were agreeing to. This means most people who are running spyware don't know exactly what it does. And since we're dealing with software which monitors your web browsing, this raises some serious concerns. For example, have you inadvertently given the spyware permission to monitor your online banking transactions? Can it keep track of the credit card numbers you enter when you shop online?

Arguably, as we mentioned above, a program that abused your personal details would qualify as malware rather than spyware. But if you don't know exactly what's running on your system, you've no way of knowing how malicious it is. Under the circumstances, the only safe approach is to assume the worst, and treat all spyware as if it were as dangerous as a regular virus or Trojan.

DEMOTES VALUABLE CONTENT Whichever search engine you use, it's likely you've chosen it because it consistently returns the information you want at the top of the search results. When spyware interferes with your search results, the top hit may become a dodgy commercial site, or a page of information copied and pasted from Wikipedia, plastered all about with adverts. It's a frustrating waste of time, and if you're in a rush there's a chance you'll come away with incomplete or wrong information from an illicitly promoted site.

The same principle applies when it comes to adverts. Even without spyware on your system, advertisers all over the web will try to "follow you" and show adverts that are relevant to sites you've recently visited. But advertisers that use spyware to promote their goods are likely to have a much narrower range of products to promote, meaning you're likely to see the same handful of adverts on every site, regardless of what your interests are. Spyware can thus prevent you from seeing adverts and offers you're genuinely interested in.

If you don't know exactly what's running, you've no way of knowing how malicious it is

LEADS YOU TO SHADY SITES If you click on a link or an advert that's been placed on your system by spyware, there's no telling where you'll end up. It's possible that the site it leads to may be perfectly kosher. But promotion via spyware isn't exactly a respectable business model, so there's a higher than average chance you may end up on a scam site, or one of dubious legality. Even if the site is a legitimate commercial site, its prices and service may well be uncompetitive – why else would it resort to spyware?

Unfortunately, as we've mentioned, when you arrive at such a site you may not realise you've been led there by spyware. So if you're considering making a purchase, it's vital always to go through the online checks we describe on p48 to verify its *bona fides*. And – we can't repeat this often enough – make sure you're using up-to-date antivirus software. This should detect and remove spyware before it can steer you towards any iffy sites. And even if it doesn't kill the spyware, it will protect your PC if you end up at a site that tries to trick you with a Trojan, or exploit your browser with a drive-by download.

A GUIDE TO THE MOST NOTORIOUS SPYWARE

Some pieces of spyware have managed to spread so widely they've become infamous. Here are some of the worst offenders.

BONZIBUDDY

BonziBUDDY was a purple gorilla who sat on your desktop and did various cute things such as telling jokes and singing songs. Behind the scenes, however, the BonziBUDDY software was also tracking users' web browsing habits, launching pop-up adverts and periodically resetting the user's home page to Bonzi's own site. Unsavoury behaviour from a character who had evidently been designed to appeal to children.

RATING

IRRITATION	●●●●○
SNEAKINESS	●●●●○
PREVALENCE	●●●●○
OVERALL	●●●●○

CYDOOR

Cydoor is a system that inserts adverts into other programs. There's no attempt at hijacking your PC: the program itself must be designed to support Cydoor. But Cydoor is unpopular for the way it makes advertising ubiquitous, and for the fact that it can't normally be removed without uninstalling the ad-supported application as well. For this reason, many antivirus packages will recognise Cydoor as adware and remove it.

RATING

IRRITATION	●●○○○
SNEAKINESS	●●○○○
PREVALENCE	●●○○○
OVERALL	●●○○○

EXPERT TIP ▼

Most of the spyware on these pages dates from the heyday of Windows 98 and XP. Since then, improvements in operating system and browser security have all but neutralised these particular threats. But the spyware risk hasn't gone away: hackers are still hard at work finding ways to mess with your internet settings and spy on your browsing.

COOLWEBSEARCH

There have been many versions of the CoolWebSearch browser plug-in, but all of them interfere with your web searches. One variant, for example, automatically redirects all attempts to search with Google or Yahoo! so that they instead go through CoolWebSearch's own site, giving the operator complete control over the results. It also tries to prevent you from removing it, hiding deep in your system and offering no uninstallation routine. And, as the icing on the cake, it also downloads and installs other items of adware and malware.

RATING

IRRITATION	●●●●○
SNEAKINESS	●●●●○
PREVALENCE	●●●○○
OVERALL	●●●●○

HUNTBAR

HuntBar gets onto your PC as a drive-by download – no quasi-legal licence agreements here – and attaches a toolbar to Internet Explorer and Windows Explorer. Once installed, the program displays pop-up advertisements, changes your default home page and search page and sends back all sorts of details about your web browsing to its operators, including the names of all the sites you visit – even if you go into the program's options and turn it off. Like CoolWebSearch, HuntBar can also install other software on your PC.

RATING

IRRITATION	●●●●●
SNEAKINESS	●●●●●
PREVALENCE	●●●●○
OVERALL	●●●●●

Parental control software automatically blocks content it thinks isn't suitable for kids, but the final say lies with you.

websites. So, for example, you could allow the use of a web browser during homework time to access information sites such as Wikipedia; but games would be banned until after dinner. If there's a program you particularly don't want your children using – such as a peer-to-peer client that's typically used for downloading pirated software and media – you can ban it altogether.

BLOCK CERTAIN MEDIA There's a huge range of TV shows, video clips and entire movies available online for direct download. Not all of these are suitable for minors. If the media has an age rating, you can configure many media players, including Windows Media Player, to refuse to play it when a child is logged on to the PC. If you have a shared library of media files in your home, you can tag these files yourself, to specify which ones may be streamed to the child's computer.

MANAGE WEBSITE ACCESS Perhaps the best known function of parental control software, this feature allows you to restrict the types of website your child is allowed to access. Most parental control software comes with an extensive database of sites containing potentially objectionable content, ranging from sex to "hate speech", violence, drugs and gambling. If the user tries to visit a website that hasn't been categorised, the parental control software will scan the content of the page before displaying it, and apply a provisional categorisation according to any keywords that are found.

If you're allowing a young child to use the internet it makes sense to block all but the most anodyne sites: you might even apply a "whitelist", blocking access to all sites except those you've explicitly authorised. If you've a maturing teenager in your household, however, you might allow them to have access to information on topics such as sexual relationships and drug abuse. Parental control tools will normally let you fine-tune which categories are blocked for which computer user, with predefined suggestions for children of different ages.

You can also configure your own "blacklist", specifying pages that are always blocked for everyone.

If a child finds a page blocked which they believe should be accessible, they can click a button to ask for it be unblocked – a request which will be stored for you to review at your next convenience.

WEBSITE ACCESS REPORTS It's not just access requests that will be brought to your attention. Many packages keep a record of all the websites your children are accessing, so you can keep a watchful eye on exactly what they're viewing online. You can

Many packages keep a record of all the websites your children are accessing

also browse a record of which websites they've tried to access which have been blocked by the parental control software. Armed with this information, you might choose to unblock a site which looks like something your child might have a legitimate interest in, even if they haven't explicitly requested it. Alternatively, if it's a particularly concerning site, you might want to ask them where they found the link!

Of course, it should go without saying that monitoring your child's online activity could be perceived as "prying", or as an expression of distrust. If you're going to use an activity monitoring feature like this, we recommend you talk to your children first and make sure they understand what's being recorded, and why.

MANAGE CONTACTS Children spend a huge amount of time using social networks and messaging services. It's only natural for parents to be concerned about who their children are communicating with. Though it's extremely rare for children to be abducted or "groomed" by people they meet online, it does occasionally happen. Some parental control software can monitor messages on Facebook and popular chat clients and keep a record of who your child's communicating with. It can also, if you choose, block messages from certain individuals, or prohibit communications with anyone who isn't on an approved whitelist, to ensure suspicious strangers can't contact your child.

RESTRICT OUTGOING INFORMATION The tiny (but alarming) possibility of abduction isn't the only danger in social networks and messaging services. Another risk is the possibility of your children giving away information that's useful to criminals. For example, an impostor masquerading as a friend might pop up on an internet chat service and ask a child for his or her family address. Then, he might steer the conversation onto upcoming holidays. As a worldly adult you'd immediately recognise this as very suspicious behaviour, suggesting your home is being cased for a burglary. A trusting child, however, might more easily be persuaded to give away some very compromising information.

Some parental control suites therefore let you specify certain items of information – your address, phone number or any other detail you choose – that shouldn't be communicated over email, social networking sites or instant messages. With this feature enabled, all outgoing communications are scanned before they're sent: messages containing sensitive information may be blocked, or the information may simply be removed. You can also use this feature to prevent your credit card details being transmitted over the internet by anyone other than you. If you have kids it shouldn't be necessary to explain why this is a good idea!

LOCK DOWN YOUR SETTINGS
As we've mentioned in previous chapters, modern malware attacks often rely on tricking you into actively installing a Trojan or a spyware program. As an adult, you hopefully won't fall for this – at least not after reading this book! – but kids are likely to be less aware of the dangers of installing downloads from unfamiliar sources, and more likely

to be taken in by the lure of free software. This is bad news if your family uses a shared PC: a password-stealing Trojan that's installed by your child could harvest *your* personal details the next time you log on.

Parental control software may therefore prevent kids from installing new software, and from removing existing programs (such as antivirus clients). It may also lock down other system settings, so you don't come back to your PC and find your sober desktop has been replaced by pink ponies.

An additional good reason for disabling access to system settings is that it dissuades children from trying to circumvent your parental controls. In many households, the kids are the technical experts, and may be quite adept at finding ways to subvert the protections you've put in place. Preventing them from accessing the system settings makes this harder. It may be frustrating for them, but their own safety – not to mention the security of your family PC – is at stake.

HOW TO SET WINDOWS 7 PARENTAL CONTROLS

Windows 7 comes with several built-in and bundled controls you can use to keep your kids safe. Here's how to set them up.

1 ▶ **ACTIVATING PARENTAL CONTROLS**
In the Windows 7 Control Panel you'll see an option labelled "Set up parental controls for any user". Select this and you'll be prompted to choose which user you want to apply the controls to: if your child doesn't have his or her own account, create one now and click on its icon. You'll then see a window showing the state of parental controls for this user. Click "On, enforce current settings" to activate controls.

2 ▶ **TIME LIMITS**
Click the top icon to set time limits when this account can use the computer. Limits can be applied on an hour-by-hour basis throughout the week. Hours when the user is allowed to log on are shown in white: by default no restrictions are applied. To block out an hour, click on it with the mouse, or drag to block out a region of time. Click or drag again to cancel the block and permit an hour.

3 ▶ **GAME CONTROLS**
Click on "Games" in the main Parental Controls panel to choose whether this user is allowed to play games. If he or she is, you can choose to restrict them to games rated for a certain age group, according to their Pan-European Game Information ratings and/or their BBFC certificates. Games with no ratings can be blocked or allowed by default, and you can also choose to explicitly block or allow particular games installed on the system.

4 ▶ **BLOCK SPECIFIC PROGRAMS**
By default, users can run all programs, but with a click you can set your child's account to "only use the programs I allow". When you select this, Windows will churn away for a few minutes and produce a list of all installed applications. This will include lots of unfamiliar system programs: don't worry about those. Just tick the programs you recognise and want your child to be able to use.

HOW LONG?
Setting everything up for the first time takes a little while, especially if you need to create multiple user accounts.

HOW HARD?
The Family Safety interface holds your hand pretty much every step of the way.

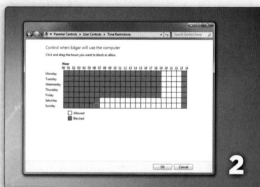

5 ▶ SETTING UP FAMILY SAFETY

Online controls are handled by the free Windows Live Family Safety add-on. To install it, find "Go online to get Windows Live Essentials" in the Control Panel and follow the prompts. If your child uses his or her own PC you'll need to install it on their computer as well. Family Safety is a network-based service, so you and your children will each need a Windows Live account. Settings are applied through a website at familysafety.live.com. (You can access the regular Parental Control settings from here too.)

6 ▶ WEB FILTERING

The first option you'll see under your child's name (at the left-hand side of the page) is web filtering. The strictest mode blocks everything but child-friendly sites, while the most lax permits all communications. You can also enable or disable web downloads here. To allow or block access to specific websites, click the "Web filtering lists" tab at the left of the screen. If your child requests access to a site you've blocked, you can review the request by clicking on "Requests" at the left of the page.

7 ▶ ACTIVITY REPORTING

Your second option is activity reporting. Click on this and you'll see a summary of your child's computer usage. Click the Web activity tab for a breakdown of which sites were visited, and which sites were blocked. If you want to block a website from this list, or allow a blocked one, you can do it from the drop-down at the right of the window. Tick "Show sites accessed by non-browser apps" and you can also see network activity from chat programs, online games and the like. Checking these logs regularly could even expose a Trojan or spyware sending data back to its creator. Under the PC activity tab you can also see when the child was using the computer, what programs they ran and what files they downloaded.

8 ▶ REQUESTS

The Requests tab lets you see if your children have requested access to any blocked sites. You can allow or block each one, for that chlld or for everyone. You can also unblock a site instantly if you're browsing with your children: simply enter your parental password when prompted.

EXPERT TIP ▼

When Family Safety is active, it activates the "safe search" features of Google, Bing and other search engines, so as to exclude dangerous and explicit sites from search results. It also disables Internet Explorer's "InPrivate" browsing mode, which ordinarily allows you to surf the web without keeping any record of the sites you visit.

▶ PARENTAL CONTROL SOFTWARE CAN HELP KEEP YOUR KIDS ON THE STRAIGHT AND NARROW, BUT SOMETIMES MORE ACTIVE MEASURES ARE APPROPRIATE.

Keeping kids safe online

WE'VE DESCRIBED WHAT parental control software does, and how you can set it up, but it's important to realise that this isn't a "set and forget" solution. If you want your children to be safe online, you need to be actively involved in what they're doing on their computers, and in how they're using the internet. On these pages we'll show you some of the issues you should be aware of.

CIRCUMVENTION It may be that your kids are paragons of obedience and good behaviour. It's more likely, though, that the moment you finish setting up the software that limits their ability to use the internet, they'll start looking for ways to get round it. You can't really blame them for this – it's human nature. But for everyone's sake it's best if you don't make it easy for them.

One basic measure you can take to prevent your parental controls being circumvented is to ensure your children have only standard user accounts on any PCs they use. Even if they have their own desktop or laptop, you should be the only administrator. Otherwise they can simply uninstall the parental control software – and they can also inadvertently install viruses, Trojans and other online nasties.

Even with a standard user account, they're likely to look for ways to get around your parental control software. It's a good idea to do a few web searches yourself for terms such as "disable Windows Live Family Safety" or "get around parental controls", so you can find out about any vulnerabilities and know what to look out for. If your household uses an internet security suite that includes parental controls, consider

using this instead of Windows' built-in protections: since fewer people are likely to use this particular suite, it may be harder for your kids to find out about any loopholes it might have.

It's important to realise, however, that if your child is really determined to get out onto the unfiltered internet, he or she may well find a way – see the panel to the right. Ultimately, if you want to ensure your child is safe online, the best you can do is explain the dangers, and why you've put restrictions in place. Your child should feel safe to come to you if they come across something troubling or suspicious, even if they find it by doing something they shouldn't.

EXPERT TIP ▾

Some domestic routers have built-in parental controls, enabling you to restrict internet access for specific users or computers to certain times of day, and to block certain types of sites. This is much harder for a child to get around than software running on a local PC, so it may be worth an investment in hardware.

Kids are naturally curious, and love to test boundaries, so don't be surprised if your tech-savvy teenager seeks – and finds – ways to get around parental controls.

PARENTAL CONTROL LOOPHOLES

CYBER-BULLYING Every parent should be aware of the danger of "cyber-bullying" – a very modern form of bullying in which antagonists torment their victim with abusive messages and threats from afar, via instant messages and social networks. If your child seems upset or scared about something online, it's possible this could be the cause.

If your child does turn out to be a victim of cyber-bullying, the solution could be as simple as creating a new email address and instant messaging ID for your child, one the bullies don't know about. If the problem persists, encourage your child to keep records of what happens and when, so you can take the matter up with parents, school staff or even the local authorities.

If you want to learn more about cyber-bullying, and what to do if it affects your child, visit the government's information page via www.pcpro.co.uk/links/cyber-bullying.

LEGAL CONSIDERATIONS Kids love to download games, movies and music. Unfortunately, they rarely have the money to pay for them; so pirated software and unauthorised downloads are hugely attractive. The most common way to access these files is via BitTorrent – a system which automatically shares the files you download with others. Popular BitTorrent clients include Vuze, µTorrent, Transmission and BitComet.

BitTorrent is not something you want your child to get involved with. Quite apart from the ethical issues – and the risks of illegal downloads containing malware and Trojans – there are legal considerations. If your child is caught downloading and sharing copyright material over your domestic internet connection, it's you who will be held responsible. With the law as it currently stands, you'll receive written warnings before any legal action is taken, so don't panic if you find a BitTorrent program on your child's computer: you're not in trouble just yet. But you should certainly insist that your child removes the software – and explain why.

Many parental control packages – such as Windows Live Family Safety – work on only one type of system. So long as everybody in your family uses a Windows PC, that's fine. But what if your child has a games console that connects to the internet? Or, what if they have access to an iPad? Most parental control software can't protect devices like these at all, so they represent a big hole in your security.

A resourceful teenager could circumvent your controls by booting a "live" Ubuntu Linux installation from a USB flash drive, evading Windows' security entirely. However, this won't help them if parental controls are built into the router (see tip).

Even if your router is locked down, your children may still be able to access the internet with no restrictions on their phones. The only thing you can do about this is install parental control software on their phones – see p139 for more details.

IN THIS CHAPTER

Chapter

8

SECURITY SOFT

In this chapter we turn our attention to the various software packages you can install to protect yourself against the dangers of the internet. On the pages that follow you'll find a full overview of what security software is, what it does, and why it needs constant updating. We'll also focus on some useful

 internet Security 2012

Recently protected
Issues to fix

Events
13

Settings

Auto Pilot
ON

VIRUS
days ago

FIREWALL
Current network profile:
Home/Office

ANTISPAM
Spam rate: unavailable

UPDATE
Last update: today

Network details

Manage

Update now

Firewall   ON

Antispam   ON

Auto Update   ON

Feedback   Complete registration   License Info   Help and Support   ?

WARE

security features that go beyond mere malware
detection, including advanced firewalls, online
backup systems and web page scanning. And we'll
explain some of the downsides of using security
software, to help you make an informed decision
about what you want running on your PC.

▶ SECURITY SOFTWARE IS THE ANTIDOTE TO ONLINE THREATS, EITHER REMOVING THEM FROM YOUR PC OR STOPPING THEM FROM REACHING IT IN THE FIRST PLACE.

What security software does

EXPERT TIP ▼
Some particularly virulent malware tries to disable or interfere with security scans. If you suspect foul play, try using a boot disc to scan from outside of Windows – see p23. Also consider running a scan with a different security package: different signatures and behavioural systems may catch something that yours have missed.

THERE ARE SO MANY different types of online threat that it may seem impossible to recognise and evade them all. Thankfully, it's not necessary to be an expert on every form of malware to stay safe. All you need to do is ensure you're running security software on your PC. This might be a straightforward antivirus package such as Microsoft's free Security Essentials tool; or it could be one of the numerous more sophisticated third-party alternatives – commonly referred to as "security suites", on account of their bringing together a range of different security tools. Collectively, we'll refer to antivirus software and security suites as "security software". In the next chapter we'll discuss the specifics of various products. But first, we'll start with a general look at how security software can keep your system safe from harm.

ON-DEMAND SCANNING The first job of any antivirus tool is to spot viruses and other malware. "On-demand" scanning means that, when instructed by you, the software will scour your system for malicious software and alert you if any is found. Normally you'll have the option to perform either a full scan, which will inspect every file on your system, or a quick scan, which checks only the most common hiding places for malware.

Which one you choose depends on your circumstances. A quick scan will almost always find any malware that's running on your computer, and it only takes a matter of seconds to run. A full scan is much slower – on a large hard disk with lots of files it can take upwards of fifteen minutes. But a full scan also confirms that there are no malware files sitting dormant on your PC, which you might otherwise end up running or passing on to a friend.

An on-demand scan typically recognises malware with the aid of an internal database of "signatures" – statistics such as the sizes, names and contents of files that are known to be malicious. This database needs constant updating to provide protection against the newest threats – see p90.

The database also tells the security software how to completely remove each type of malware (as painstakingly worked out by security researchers), so if a virus or Trojan is found on your system, you can erase it with the click of a button.

Real-time detection ensures you can't inadvertently open a file that's infected with malware.

AUTOMATIC SCANNING In addition to on-demand scanning, almost all security software offers some form of automatic scanning, to ensure nothing gets missed. Typically such scans are carried out to a schedule – for example, an antivirus program might perform a full scan at 3 o'clock every Wednesday morning. Scheduled scans are typically set for times when you're not likely to be using the PC, so as not to interfere with your work.

This approach has one weakness: if you switch your PC off when you're not using it, your scheduled scan might never run, and malware might linger undetected on your system. Some security software, therefore, also performs "idle scans" – checking files whenever the system appears to be unused. For example, a scan might start if no one's touched the keyboard for five minutes and CPU usage is lower than 5%. When you start using the computer again, the scan will be suspended until the computer's next idle.

It's worth noting that opening and analysing every single file on your system is an intensive process. If you're using a laptop, a full scan could have a noticeable effect on your battery life. For this reason, many security packages allow you to suspend automatic scanning when your computer's using battery power.

REAL-TIME SCANNING On-demand and scheduled scanning is all very well; but if a virus finds its way onto your system you'll probably want to know about it right away, rather than waiting for your next scan. Real-time scanning means that every time you open a program or file, your security software scans it there and then. Downloaded files are also scanned as soon as they arrive on your hard disk, ensuring malware is caught at the very earliest opportunity.

Inevitably, real-time scanning entails a certain overhead: it takes time to analyse a file and check it's not malicious, so programs take longer to load and your CPU is busier. But the impact is much smaller than you might expect. Modern security software is very efficient, so the delay in opening applications and documents is likely to be a mere second or less – and the impact on your computer's performance is normally quite unnoticeable.

BEHAVIOURAL DETECTION The malware detection methods we've referred to so far all rely on signatures. This means they can only detect threats that have been identified and analysed by security researchers. If you're caught in the first wave of a new virus outbreak, your security software might not be able to find or remove the malware on your system until it receives a database update.

Happily, there's a second tactic which can complement the signature-based approach – a tactic

A quick scan will almost always find any malware that's running on your computer

which can even identify threats that have never been seen before. This tactic is called behavioural monitoring. As the name suggests, it tries to identify malicious software on your computer simply by monitoring how programs behave. For example: if a program runs automatically each time Windows starts up, doesn't open any sort of user interface and silently sends data to servers in other countries, it's very likely to be malware, and a behavioural detection system will flag it as such.

One apparent downside of behavioural detection is that it can only analyse programs that are already installed on your PC – so your personal data may already have been compromised by the time an item of malware is identified. Some security software gets round this problem by trying out unrecognised software in a "sandbox" – a simulated, completely isolated testing environment. Only software that behaves cleanly inside the sandbox, without attempting to do anything suspicious, is allowed to launch for real, and to access your real data files and internet connection.

> (!) A nasty type of malware known as a "rootkit" tampers with your system to conceal its presence from antivirus software. This type of malware can normally be detected with a full system scan, but real-time scanning will miss it.

▶ SECURITY SOFTWARE RELIES ON INFORMATION TO DO ITS JOB – INFORMATION WHICH MUST BE KEPT CONSTANTLY UP TO DATE TO ACCOUNT FOR THE LATEST THREATS.

Understanding updates

WHEN YOU CONSIDER how security software works, it's clear that efficient and reliable malware detection requires keeping your signature database as up to date as possible. This, as you might assume, is no easy task for security software developers. But you might be surprised at just how much of a challenge it is to keep up with the bad guys.

HOW URGENT ARE UPDATES? Before we go on, take a guess at how many different variations of viruses, Trojans and worms – how many different "strains" of malware, as it were – have been detected in the past few decades. Based solely on media reports of high-profile attacks during this period, you might imagine there have been only a few dozen. By now, however, you might be coming to suspect that a lot of malware goes unnoticed by the world at large, and that the true figure is much higher – perhaps in the thousands, or even the tens of thousands.

In fact the number is still higher – and considerably so. Security researchers at Russian antivirus vendor Kaspersky Lab claim that their software currently detects around *eight million* different items of malware and unwanted software. Other security experts report similar figures.

If this number seems mind-bogglingly high,

it's partly a sobering reflection of how effectively modern malware manages to stay under the radar. However, it's worth explaining that, these days, a large proportion of the threats you might encounter online are variations on common themes.

For example, a malware creator might distribute a single piece of Trojan code in a hundred different forms – all of which work the same way, but which come bundled up in hard-to-recognise files of different sizes and types. This is sometimes called "obfuscation". With the right computer software, it's not hard to achieve, and it can greatly hinder antivirus efforts. After all, it takes time for researchers to identify a threat, create a signature for it and send out a database update so that security software users are protected against it. You can imagine how much longer it takes to provide protection against a hundred variants. Obfuscation thus buys extra time for the malware to steal passwords, infect PCs or do whatever other damage it likes, undetected.

Between genuinely new threats and obfuscated variations on existing ones, security software developers are now adding almost 10,000 new signatures to their databases *each day*. Clearly, then, updates need to be very fast and very frequent if they're to protect you against all the latest threats.

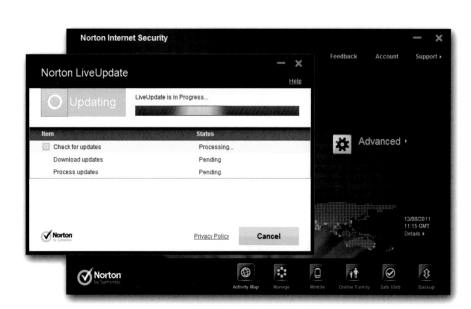

With ten thousand new signatures a day, an update mechanism is an integral part of a security suite.

Kaspersky Internet Security, like many security suites, uses a cloud-based reputation system to help it identify malware.

Most security software updates its signature database at least once a day: some packages check for updates every hour, or even maintain a constant connection to the update server to download updates the very minute they become available. More major updates are occasionally rolled out too, such as improvements to the detection engine.

THE SUBSCRIPTION MODEL All of the work involved in keeping databases up to date explains why commercial antivirus software is sold via a subscription model. The purchase price includes a certain period of updates (typically twelve months), and if you want to continue receiving updates after this you have to pay again.

If you look at the statistics you might wonder whether it's really worth maintaining a subscription beyond the first year. After all, with eight million signatures already in the database, it's very likely that if you do run into a virus it will already be covered – right?

In practice, however, it doesn't work this way. The vast majority of those eight million existing threats are designed to exploit old vulnerabilities, which have since been closed off. If you're regularly running Windows Update and applying application patches, there's a good chance your system is already protected against most of them. The real value of security software is the front-line protection it can provide against brand-new "zero day" exploits – so called because there's no opportunity to patch them before the malware strikes.

At any rate, the sellers of security software really don't want you to keep on using it without paying again. As you'll know if you've ever used commercial security software, when your subscription draws close to an end you can expect to be bombarded with reminders nagging you to extend it. If you ignore these and let your subscription expire, the software may refuse to work properly. At the very least it's likely to complain constantly, to the extent that your only realistic option may be to renew it – or remove it.

A DATABASE IN THE CLOUD In the past few years, rather than relying wholly on a database that's stored on your hard disk, modern security software has started to make use of central online databases. This approach has one big benefit: as soon as a new signature is created, it becomes available to all users. But it has one big limitation too: whenever you don't have an internet connection (for example, when you're

A malware creator might distribute a single piece of Trojan code in a hundred different forms

travelling on a plane or a cross-country train), the database won't be contactable and dangerous files could go unnoticed. The software therefore still has to maintain a local database, as a fall-back.

However, using a central database has one other advantage too: it makes it possible to aggregate information from all users. For example, if the software identifies a piece of malware through behavioural analysis on one person's PC, it can be automatically blocked on everyone else's system. The software can also estimate a file's trustworthiness – an approach called heuristic detection – based partly on its prevalence and distribution. If an unrecognised file suddenly starts popping up on lots of computers all around the world, that suggests that it should be treated with caution.

Services such as these are sometimes referred to as "cloud protection", because they're based in that airy conceptual space known as "the cloud" rather than on your PC. Maintaining access to these services is another reason why it may be worth renewing your security software subscription.

Security software developers share information, so you might expect all major packages to provide similar protection. But some produce signatures more quickly and effectively than others, as we'll see in Chapter 9.

Third-party firewalls

MANY SECURITY SUITES include a firewall – a so-called "third-party" firewall, because it replaces Microsoft's own offering. We've already explained the basics of firewalls on p58, but it's worth recapping some of the differences you can expect to see between the regular Windows firewall and a third-party one.

MORE REQUESTERS Third-party firewalls are normally two-way. This means they can block programs running on your PC from accessing the internet, as well as blocking external computers that connect to you over the network.

Depending on the firewall you choose, this could have a big effect on your experience. If you choose a "noisy" firewall – one that's configured to ask your permission for every network access request – you can expect to see dozens of requesters in your first few days, as each of the various programs on your system requests permission to access the network. (We've even seen firewalls that won't trust Internet Explorer without confirmation from you.)

This isn't as tiresome as it sounds: whenever you click to allow a program to go online, your decision will be remembered, so the barrage of requesters should soon die down. But if you don't like being pestered, or if you don't like having to make technical decisions, choose a firewall that's designed to stay in the background and make its own decisions as to what to block and what to allow.

MULTIPLE NETWORKS The Windows Firewall applies different settings depending on whether you're using a Home, Work or Public network – but these settings apply to all networks of a given type. If you travel between many different networks, and want to maintain control over your settings on each of them, you'll need a third-party firewall.

CONFIGURABILITY Third-party firewalls often allow you to create highly complex rules – for example, you might decide that a certain program is only allowed to access the internet via a certain port when connected to a certain type of network. If you're a technical type, or need to fit into a complicated network system, this could be very useful. Most of us, however, are likely to find such settings bamboozling.

**EXPERT
TIP** ▼

Some firewalls have a "learning mode" that permits all internet access for a limited time, and learns what sort of network activity is "normal" for your PC based on what happens during this period. It's a clever compromise between a noisy firewall and a silent one; but it's vital that no malware is running during the learning period, for obvious reasons!

A third-party firewall will often provide more detailed technical information than the taciturn Windows Firewall.

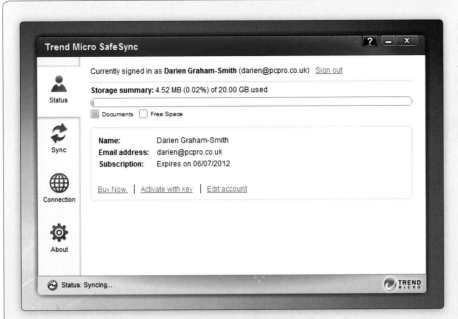

Backup tools have their uses, but be aware of their limitations before you get invested.

> **(!)** Don't try to use a file sync service like Dropbox or Windows Live Mesh as an alternative to a real backup system. These services don't keep old copies of your data: delete an important file from your Dropbox and it's gone for good.

ONLINE BACKUP:
IS IT WORTH PAYING FOR?

Some security suites include an online backup service, to keep copies of your documents safe in case disaster strikes (whether malware-related or otherwise). Invariably, though, this service comes at an extra cost. Is it worth it?

✓ **NO-FUSS PROTECTION** Keeping online backups is typically effortless: copies are made automatically whenever you update your documents. And since the backup client is part of your security software, you don't need to mess around with multiple programs.

✓ **SAFER THAN HOUSES** Because your files are stored far away from your home, you can be sure they'll survive more or less any disaster, from a Trojan attack to a flood or burglary. Your files are normally encrypted on the server, to ensure no one can hack in and access your information. And the companies operating these services are large, established organisations, so you can be confident your backups will be accessible whenever you need them.

✓ **COST EFFECTIVE** There are plenty of companies out there that specialise in online backup, and who will happily sell you an open-ended backup service. But buying a backup service as part of a year-long security suite licence can work out cheaper on a per-megabyte, per-month basis – especially if you shop around.

✗ **LIMITED SPACE** Online backup services typically include only a few gigabytes of space, and ratchet up the price sharply if you want to store more. If you have a large amount of data you want to protect – for example, if you shoot home movies – it may be more economical to look into an offline backup system, such as a dedicated external drive.

✗ **SLOW ACCESS** The speed at which you can access your online backups is limited by the speed of your internet connection. This isn't a problem if you only want to protect a few documents and images. But if you have many gigabytes of data to protect, it can take a very long time to upload it all to the backup service – and it'll take a considerable time to retrieve all that data should you ever need it.

✗ **DIFFICULT TO MOVE** Once you've uploaded your data to an online backup service, it's a pain to switch to a different provider, should you wish to do so. This is true of all online backup services, but it's a particular concern if your backup service is tied to your security suite subscription. Should you ever decide to move to a different security package (or stop using a commercial suite altogether), you'll have to make alternative backup arrangements as well. If you use an independent backup service, the problem simply doesn't arise.

Web page and link scanning

As we mentioned in Chapter 1, traditional viruses make up only a small proportion of current malware. The underground nature of malware makes it impossible to give precise figures, but we can say with confidence that in your everyday browsing there's a much greater risk that you'll run into a Trojan, lurking on a web page, than any other sort of threat.

The popularity of Trojans is no surprise. This type of malware is very easy to create – and, because it's distributed directly from a web server, it's easy to obfuscate and change on a daily basis, making it difficult for antivirus software to reliably detect it.

In other words, even if you're using a reputable security suite with the latest signatures, a Trojan could still slip under its defences and infect your PC. Hopefully such an intrusion would be rapidly spotted by other methods, such as behavioural detection or reputation analysis, as we discussed. But to make sure nothing gets through, many security packages also employ another type of detection – one that doesn't rely at all on recognising the content of the Trojan, or its behaviour.

WEB SCANNING Web scanning is a malware defence system that warns you whenever you visit a web page that's known to harbour dangerous code – or one that appears to be a scam.

In its simplest implementation, a web scanning module might appear as a toolbar in your browser, showing alerts of various colours as you browse. A green light would mean that the site has been verified as safe, and you can browse and download files with confidence. A yellow light would typically be a warning that the site had no history of malicious behaviour, but was nevertheless considered suspicious (we'll discuss possible reasons for this below). A red light would indicate that you were visiting a site that was known to be dangerous.

How are these ratings determined? Well, different web scanners use different systems. Almost all of them maintain a database of sites that have been known in the past to actively distribute malware. This enables them to warn you that a site is dangerous as soon as you arrive there, without having to wait for it to try to infect your PC. Malware isn't the only

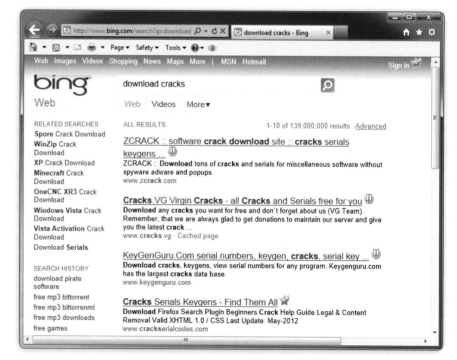

A link scanning system adds helpful icons to search results, showing which sites are safe and which might not be trustworthy.

Web scanning steps in when you click on a link to a site that's known – or suspected – to be dangerous.

reason a site might be considered dangerous: security researchers will also try to catalogue confirmed scam sites (see Chapter 2), so a web scanner can warn you that the page you're using doesn't appear to be legit.

What if you visit a page that hasn't been indexed? A web scanner may look at circumstantial data, such as the age of a website and where it's based. Scam sites tend to be short-lived, to evade detection, and based in countries where law enforcement agencies have shown little interest in pursuing cyber-crimes. If you wind up on a page in Uzbekistan which has only been in existence for a few hours, that might be enough to trigger a yellow alert.

These methods can also be partnered with a direct analysis of the web page's code. As we've mentioned, the ever-changing nature of Trojans means it's not always possible for security software to recognise the hosted malware itself. Instead, some web scanners look for the presence of drive-by download code – that is, the specific routines that trick your web browser into installing a Trojan without your permission. This code is difficult for the malware creator to obfuscate, as it needs to work in a certain way for the exploit to work. You may therefore find that your web scanner throws up a warning whenever you visit a page that has the *capacity* to infect you, whether or not that capacity is used.

INTERSTITIALS AND LINK SCANNING We noted in Chapter 1 that some Trojans work by persuading you to download and install an innocent-looking file. A site that distributes malware in this way will be flagged as dangerous by most web scanners, although you can browse around it quite safely so long as you don't download anything.

However, there's no way of telling whether a site might also try to infect your PC with a drive-by download. The best way to stay safe, therefore, is never to visit a dangerous site in the first place.

For this reason, if you try to visit a site that's known to be dangerous, many web scanners will intercept the connection and throw up a warning page, sometimes called an "interstitial" warning. If you're certain you want to visit the site, you can

normally click a link to proceed, but the recommended action is always to go back to somewhere safe.

Some scanners give you an earlier warning by also placing safety ratings next to your results in web search engines like Google and Bing – an approach called "link scanning". For example, if you're searching for "free games", you'll be able to see at a glance which sites have a good reputation and which have been associated with malware. There's no need to click the links to expose dangerous sites – you can simply skip

Some scanners place safety ratings next to your results in web search engines

right over them. A few security suites (such as Norton Internet Security – see p116) take this idea further and also provide trust information for online shopping sites, so you can see at a glance, for example, what type of security an online store uses, and what its reputation is.

LIMITATIONS OF WEB SCANNING Web scanning relies partly on a site's existing reputation. This means that if a hacker manages to break into someone else's site and embed a drive-by download on a respected page, your web scanner could continue to give the site a green light – at least, until the malware is spotted.

This isn't a fanciful idea: it's happened many times. In 2007, a hacker in the US managed to insert a key-logging Trojan onto the official page of Miami's Dolphin Stadium, the venue for that year's Super Bowl. And in late 2011, the home page of MySQL.com (a popular open-source database system) was hacked in a similar way. While web scanning is a valuable system, it's certainly not a replacement for active malware detection.

WE'VE DESCRIBED THE MAJOR FUNCTIONS OF SECURITY SOFTWARE, BUT MANY
PACKAGES INCLUDE ADDITIONAL TOOLS FOR PROTECTING YOUR PC AND YOUR DATA.

Additional features

YOU CAN TAKE IT as read that an antivirus program
or a security suite will detect malware and spyware
– as we discussed on p88, that's "job one". Most
security suites will probably contain a firewall and
a web scanning module as well. But in addition to
the mainstream features we've already discussed,
some packages offer extra tools and settings, to
provide extra protection or convenience – and to set
themselves apart from the pack. On these pages we'll
explain some of these secondary security features.

NETWORK MONITORING If an intruder manages
to connect to your home network, they may be able
to access your personal data, or even install malware
on your computers. On p62 we described various
measures you can take to keep strangers out. Some
security software provides an extra layer of protection
by monitoring all the computers and devices on your
network, and alerting you whenever anything new
connects. In some cases network monitoring can also
be used to manage antivirus software across multiple
machines: you can check at a glance whether any of
the computers in your household is using an out-of-

date version of the security software, or whether it's
installed at all. You may even be able to remedy this
automatically, ensuring there are no weak spots in
your home security.

GAME/MOVIE MODE If you're watching a film
or playing a game on your PC, you don't want to be
pestered with popups. Even if a potentially suspicious
file is found, there's no need to handle it there and
then. Many security suites will automatically switch
into a silent "game mode", or "movie mode", whenever
they detect that you're using an application with a
full-screen view. Some software may also dial back its
CPU and network usage, so as not to interfere if you're
playing a game.

PERSONAL INFORMATION MONITOR As we
mentioned on p80, some parental control software
allows you to prevent certain pieces of information
(such as credit card numbers) from being sent from
your PC out onto the internet. This isn't only useful
in the context of parental controls: it can also prevent
information-stealing Trojans from transmitting their

EXPERT TIP ▾

If your chosen
security suite
doesn't include
all the secondary
features you want,
don't despair: many
of these jobs can be
done by standalone
software. We've
already mentioned
LastPass (see p52);
search the web
and you'll also
find plenty of free
sandbox tools,
encryption utilities
and file shredders.

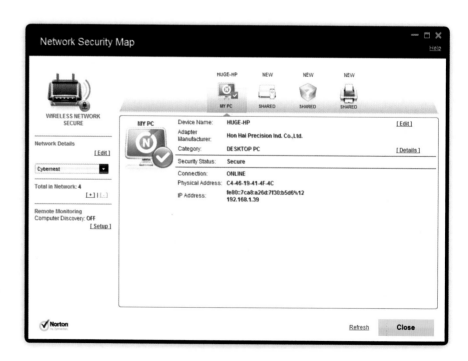

Some suites let you
keep track of all
the devices on your
home network,
and manage their
security settings.

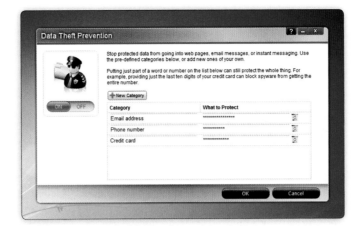

Monitoring outgoing traffic for sensitive information can protect you from password-stealing Trojans and other unwanted intrusions.

ill-gotten data back to their creators. Some security software monitors your outgoing traffic for confidential information, and will require your explicit permission before any of your personal information can be sent to a remote server. If you're making an online purchase, you can click to authorise – otherwise it's time to block the connection and scan for malware.

PASSWORD MANAGER On p52 we showed you how to install and use the free LastPass password manager. If you're using a commercial security suite, however, this may not be necessary: some suites come with their own built-in password managers. This makes it easy for you to use secure, unguessable passwords – and also provides a degree of protection against "key loggers", which try to steal passwords by monitoring what you type.

SAFE BROWSER One novel feature you may see is a "safe browser" – that is, a web browser that's designed to provide better security than a regular one. This isn't to say that normal web browsers are unsafe: so long as you're using the latest version of a mainstream browser such as Internet Explorer, Chrome, Firefox or Safari for your everyday browsing, you should have a good degree of protection against online attacks.

A safe browser, however, applies much stricter security rules – rules so strict, in fact, that you might find it a pain to use for regular browsing. For example, you might be asked to provide explicit permission when a site wants to store a cookie on your PC, or when it wants to show an embedded Flash video.

The idea is that you use this browser when you're visiting a site you might not trust – for example, when following a link that's been sent to you by email. Many things the site tries to do may be denied by default, unless you explicitly authorise them, making it very hard for malicious code to infect your PC. The site may also be blocked off from downloading files to your PC or accessing information about your system, again heading off possible avenues of attack. And any information that is downloaded will be completely isolated from the rest of your system.

Keeping your data safe isn't just about protecting it from destructive malware

SANDBOX On p89 we mentioned that a sandbox is a safe, simulated testing environment, which can be used to find out what a program does without giving it full access to your system. Some programs use sandboxing techniques for behavioural detection, but often you'll also have the option of running any program you like in a sandbox – so you can see for yourself what it does, without putting the safety of your system and your personal information at risk. If someone you don't know well sends you an executable file, it's a good idea to try it out in a sandbox before installing it for real.

FILE ENCRYPTION Keeping your data safe isn't just about protecting it from destructive malware. If you have confidential information on your PC, you may want to be absolutely sure that no one can gain access to it – even if your laptop is lost or stolen. Some security software includes encryption functions that you can use to ensure just that. With modern encryption methods, even if someone gets hold of your files they will be unable to read them without knowing your secure password. We'll talk more about encryption in Chapter 10.

FILE SHREDDING Encrypting your confidential data is an important aspect of data protection, but it's also worth thinking about what happens to sensitive files after you delete them. In many cases, the information they contain could be recoverable by someone who gains access to your hard disk. To prevent this, a security suite might include so-called "shredding" tools that completely wipe selected files from the disk, ensuring they can't be recovered. Again, we'll return to this topic in Chapter 10.

The ultimate sandbox is a complete virtual machine, on which you can run anything you like in safety. Setting this up isn't for beginners, but if you want to try it you'll find free virtualisation software at www. virtualbox.org.

▶ WITHOUT A DOUBT IT'S A GOOD IDEA TO RUN SECURITY SOFTWARE – BUT DOING SO
CAN INVOLVE SOME COSTS, AND SOME COMPROMISES TO PC PERFORMANCE.

The downsides of security software

IT OUGHT TO BE clear by now that, if you want to be safe online, a security suite can help enormously. However, there's no such thing as a free lunch, and there are a few possible catches to using this type of software.

A PRICE TO PAY Not all security software costs money: as we'll detail in the next chapter, some quite effective antivirus clients can be had for free. However, if you want the best features and the maximum protection, you'll have to look to a commercial package, which means committing to a regular subscription fee.

The cost doesn't have to break the bank. You may be able to save money by buying a multi-year subscription, rather than the more common twelve-month deal. And if you have several PCs to protect you can often save a lot of money by buying a multi-licence pack. Ultimately, though, if you choose a commercial security suite, you're going to have to pay for it. And if you use a free alternative, you may find you're pestered with advertising. After all, maintaining and updating a database of millions of malware samples costs money, and it has to come from somewhere.

A BEWILDERING CHOICE Choice can be good, but when it comes to picking security software there's an overwhelming range of options, each with its own combination of features and its own strengths and weaknesses. In the next chapter we'll describe some of the major titles: but because the fight against malware is an ever-changing field, the comparative effectiveness of each one may change over time. Before you invest, check a respected reviews site such as www.pcpro.co.uk for impartial, up-to-date advice.

IMPACT ON PERFORMANCE It's sometimes claimed that antivirus software will slow your PC to a crawl. This is a myth. It's true that checking files for malware does take some time, and it does use up some memory; but on a modern PC the effect should be wholly unnoticeable. If you want to check the "weight" of a security program, the steps on the opposite page will provide a rough and ready measure of its impact (run the first three steps both before and after installing the software). But what's really important is responsiveness: if your PC doesn't feel any slower with the security software installed, there's no harm done.

**EXPERT
TIP** ▼

When you subscribe to a commercial security package, you might be invited to sign up for automatic renewal in twelve months' time. If you decline this, you may well be offered a cheaper renewal option when the time comes. It may also work out cheaper simply to buy a new copy of the software when yours expires.

You can often save money by buying a subscription for multiple PCs.

MEASURING THE IMPACT OF SECURITY SOFTWARE

1 ▶ **TIME TO BOOT**
Security software needs to be loaded into memory while your computer's starting up, so the first thing to check is how much time it adds to your regular boot procedure. You can measure this with a stopwatch – simply start timing when you press the power button, and stop when the desktop or logon prompt appears. To get a fair average reading you should try this a few times before installing the software, then again a few times once it's installed.

2 ▶ **CPU USAGE AFTER BOOT**
Many security programs continue to initialise even after the desktop has appeared. This could get in the way while you're trying to open and use applications. An easy way to see what's going on is to open the Windows Task Manager – you can do this by typing "Task Manager" at the Start menu, or by pressing Ctrl+Shift+Esc. Click the "Performance" tab and you'll see a readout of CPU usage. Open this as soon as Windows boots, and don't open any other programs: you can now compare post-boot CPU usage before and after installing the security software.

3 ▶ **MEMORY USAGE**
To offer real-time protection, security software must stay in memory at all times. Again, you can measure the impact of this using the Task Manager: RAM usage is displayed directly below CPU usage. Start by finding the memory "footprint" of your system without the security software installed: boot your system, open the Task Manager, and don't run any programs. Wait two or three minutes – this is how long it takes for all of Windows' startup tasks to complete. The memory usage you see will then be your baseline. Install the security software and repeat the process to see how much extra RAM is used.

4 ▶ **INTRUSIVENESS**
This is the one aspect of performance that can't be measured. Interruptions such as firewall requests and subcription reminders can be annoying, and can even negatively affect your productivity; but the scale of the problem depends on your personal preferences, and the way you use your PC. The best way to find out if a security package is too intrusive for you is simply to try it out before you buy.

> **(!)** These tests give an idea of security software's impact on your system, but they're not really scientific: Windows is a multi-tasking operating system, so other processes running in the background could skew your results.

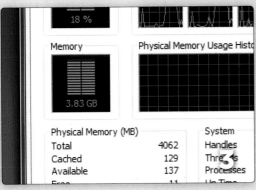

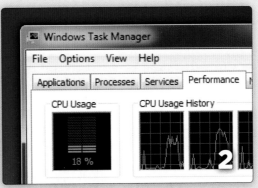

IN THIS CHAPTER

Chapter

9

CHOOSING A SE

You understand the importance of security software. But which suite do you choose? It's a crowded market out there, and there are so many factors to consider, from protection levels to features and price. In this chapter we'll give you an overview of nine of the biggest and best-known packages to

CURITY SUITE

help you decide. Note that security companies are continually updating their software, and many suites are offered in multiple versions, such as antivirus-only packages, or premium bundles that include online backup. Check the developer's website before you get out your credit card!

▶ MICROSOFT'S OWN SECURITY SOFTWARE COMES FREE WITH WINDOWS AND RECEIVES REGULAR UPDATES. IF YOU'RE A CASUAL COMPUTER USER IT MAY BE ALL YOU NEED.

Microsoft Security Essentials

If you're looking for basic malware protection, a good place to start is with Microsoft Security Essentials. This antivirus program from the makers of Windows lacks fancy features: it simply runs in the background and intercepts known malware when it arrives on your system. Some people like this simplicity, however, and its clean interface makes it easy to see what's

going on, and to change settings should you wish to. One downside is that it's not updated as frequently as other security suites: new signatures are received only when you run Windows Update, which could be once a week or even less often. In PC Pro's security software tests, Security Essentials protected a test PC against 92% of malware – a good score, but not perfect.

TEST RESULTS

92%
Malware protection score in *PC Pro*'s independent tests

96%
Legitimate software allowed to run without interruption

196 MB
Added to Windows' memory usage after installation

SCORES EXPLAINED
Tests were carried out using a current version of the software during Q1 2012. The first figure reflects the software's ability to protect a test PC against an independent selection of real-world malware samples. The second indicates how many legitimate applications, again from an independent selection, ran correctly without the software interfering, raising an alert or seeking the user's permission. The third figure represents the software's overall memory footprint, as measured via the method described on p99.

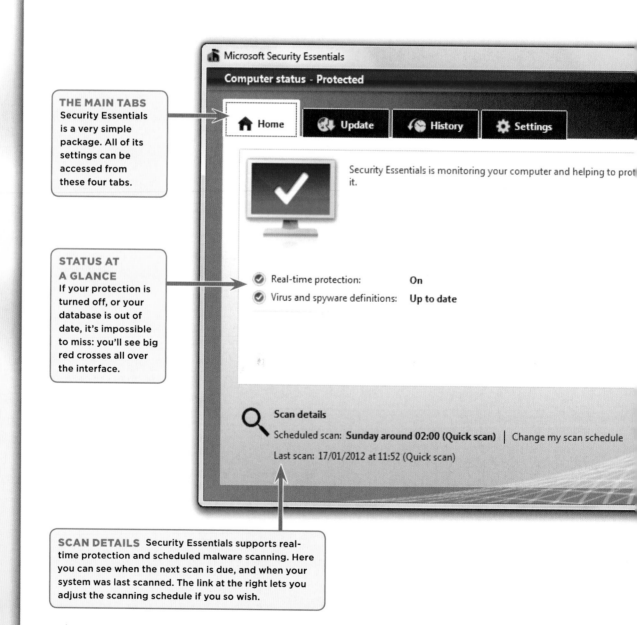

THE MAIN TABS Security Essentials is a very simple package. All of its settings can be accessed from these four tabs.

STATUS AT A GLANCE If your protection is turned off, or your database is out of date, it's impossible to miss: you'll see big red crosses all over the interface.

SCAN DETAILS Security Essentials supports real-time protection and scheduled malware scanning. Here you can see when the next scan is due, and when your system was last scanned. The link at the right lets you adjust the scanning schedule if you so wish.

KEY INFORMATION

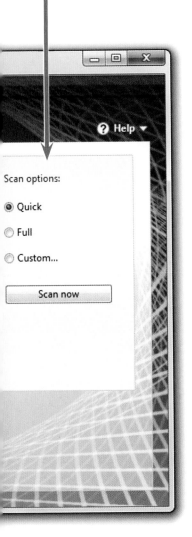

WHERE TO GET IT	
Developer's website	www.microsoft.com
PRICING	
RRP for 1 PC (12 months)	Free
RRP for 3 PCs (12 months)	Free
Free trial available?	N/A
Windows versions supported	Windows 8, 7, Vista, XP
FEATURES	
Firewall	✗
Email scanning	✗
Web protection	✗
Anti-spam	✗
Online backup	✗
Parental controls	✗
Game mode	✗
Data protection	✗
Other features	✗

◀ Security Essentials is available to download free from the Microsoft website, or you can install it as an "Optional update" through the Windows Update system. Microsoft also plans to build it directly into Windows 8, under the name "Windows Defender". As you can see from our feature table, Security Essentials is a very stripped-down package – hence the title. Under the circumstances a 196MB memory footprint is on the large side. But Security Essentials does a decent job of the basics, and you can't argue with the price.

Details in this table are subject to change. Prices stated are from the developer's website: you may be able to save money by buying from an independent retailer.

▶ When Security Essentials detects a threat, it will show an "alert level" indicating how dangerous it is. In the program's settings you can specify a default action for each different threat level - or just accept Microsoft's recommendations.

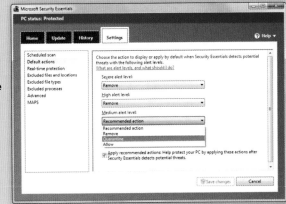

▶ THE OLDEST AND MOST POPULAR FREE ANTIVIRUS SOFTWARE STILL PROVIDES GREAT
MALWARE PROTECTION – THOUGH THE ADVERTS MIGHT PUT YOU OFF.

AVG Anti-Virus Free

IF SECURITY ESSENTIALS doesn't appeal, AVG's free antivirus package is a popular alternative. This Czech-based company has been offering free security software for more than a decade, and has a well-deserved reputation for effectiveness: in *PC Pro*'s tests, AVG Anti-Virus Free achieved an impressive 98% malware protection score, significantly higher than the 92% managed by Security Essentials. AVG's software also includes a few useful features that Security Essentials lacks, making it a tempting proposition. Be warned, however, that AVG uses its free antivirus program partly as an advertising channel: while using it, you'll see plenty of adverts for the company's commercial products.

TEST RESULTS

98%
Malware protection score in *PC Pro*'s independent tests

96%
Legitimate software allowed to run without interruption

259 MB
Added to Windows' memory usage after installation

SCORES EXPLAINED
Tests were carried out using a current version of the software during Q1 2012. The first figure reflects the software's ability to protect a test PC against an independent selection of real-world malware samples. The second indicates how many legitimate applications, again from an independent selection, ran correctly without the software interfering, raising an alert or seeking the user's permission. The third figure represents the software's overall memory footprint, as measured via the method described on p99.

OVERVIEW
The main AVG interface shows you the status of your protection, and gives you direct access to the program's various modules and settings.

MY APPS
AVG's "apps" are extra paid-for features, such as parental controls and online backup. If you've bought these, you can click here to access them.

ADVERTISING
This advert, urging you to upgrade to the paid-for edition, is a constant reminder that you're using a free product.

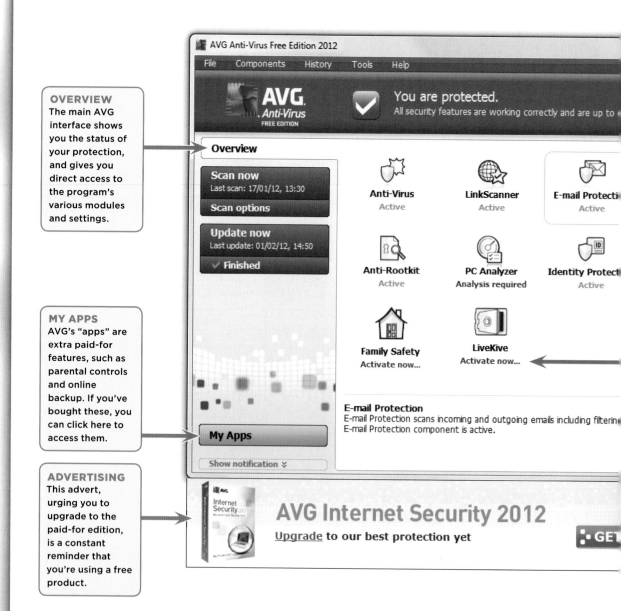

KEY INFORMATION

EMAIL PROTECTION
Like many security suites, AVG can scan incoming emails and automatically block access to malware, to protect you against worms. It can also identify and filter spam automatically.

ACTIVATE NOW
Several of the modules you'll see in the main AVG interface aren't actually included in the software. Their icons are here purely to encourage you to upgrade. See also the My Apps button, opposite.

WHERE TO GET IT	
Developer's website	http://free.avg.com
PRICING	
RRP for 1 PC (12 months)	Free
RRP for 3 PCs (12 months)	Free
Free trial available?	N/A
Windows versions supported	Windows 8, 7, Vista, XP
FEATURES	
Firewall	✗
Email scanning	✓
Web protection	✓
Anti-spam	✓
Online backup	✗
Parental controls	✗
Game mode	✓
Data protection	✗
Other features	✗

◀ AVG's free antivirus software doesn't come with much in the way of features. That might make its large 259MB memory footprint hard to swallow, but it does include a useful web protection module (see below). If you want more features you can upgrade to AVG's paid-for suite for £36 a year for one PC. You can also add on various features: the "LiveKive" online backup system costs £55 per year for unlimited storage, while AVG's Family Safety parental control system is £13 a year for a three-PC household.

Details in this table are subject to change. Prices stated are from the developer's website: you may be able to save money by buying from an independent retailer.

◀ AVG's free antivirus program includes a web protection module called LinkScanner. This integrates with your web browser and adds warnings to your web search results, helping you steer well clear of dangerous pages.

▶ Although AVG's feature set isn't huge, it offers a comprehensive range of options, making it much more configurable than Security Essentials. If you like to tweak and personalise your software, you'll find AVG gives you plenty to play with.

▶ THE INTERFACE MAY LOOK UNNERVINGLY FUTURISTIC, BUT BITDEFENDER'S SECURITY SUITE IS SUPREMELY EASY TO USE – AND HIGHLY EFFECTIVE TOO.

BitDefender Internet Security

BITDEFENDER INTERNET SECURITY has a moody, dark interface and plenty of features, including web protection, Wi-Fi network monitoring and optional free plugins to protect you from potentially dangerous content on Twitter and Facebook. But don't be daunted: it's actually one of the easiest security suites to use, thanks to its innovative "Auto Pilot"

mode. When this is switched on, BitDefender handles everything, without interrupting you at all. If you want more control, simply switch it off and you can deal with firewall requests and malware detection events yourself. Across PC Pro's tests it achieved a perfect 100% score, making it an appealing option for both novices and expert users alike.

TEST RESULTS

100%

Malware protection score in *PC Pro*'s independent tests

100%

Legitimate software allowed to run without interruption

197MB

Added to Windows' memory usage after installation

SCORES EXPLAINED

Tests were carried out using a current version of the software during Q1 2012. The first figure reflects the software's ability to protect a test PC against an independent selection of real-world malware samples. The second indicates how many legitimate applications, again from an independent selection, ran correctly without the software interfering, raising an alert or seeking the user's permission. The third figure represents the software's overall memory footprint, as measured via the method described on p99.

ANTIVIRUS
BitDefender Internet Security uses the term "virus" to mean all types of malware. As its test results show, it provides comprehensive protection against Trojans and spyware as well.

FIREWALL
BitDefender's firewall is much more configurable than the Windows Firewall, but setting up custom rules can be complex – it's best left for expert users.

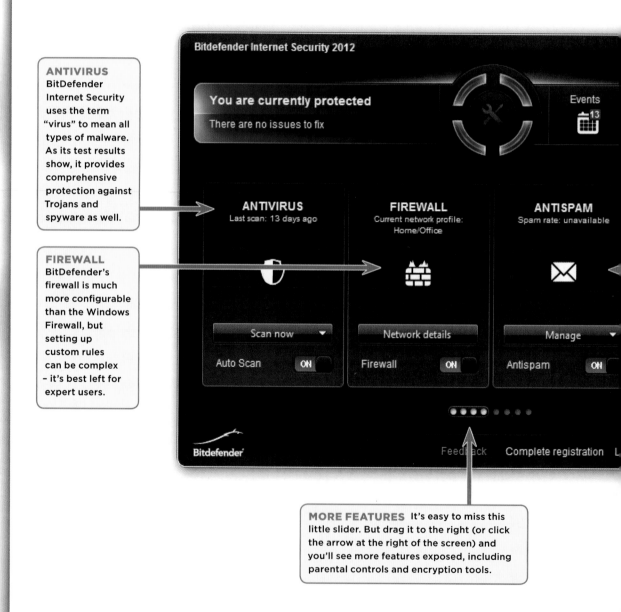

MORE FEATURES It's easy to miss this little slider. But drag it to the right (or click the arrow at the right of the screen) and you'll see more features exposed, including parental controls and encryption tools.

KEY INFORMATION

WHERE TO GET IT	
Developer's website	www.bitdefender.co.uk
PRICING	
RRP for 1 PC (12 months)	£29.99
RRP for 3 PCs (12 months)	£39.99
Free trial available?	30 days
Windows versions supported	Windows 8, 7, Vista, XP
FEATURES	
Firewall	✓
Email scanning	✓
Web protection	✓
Anti-spam	✓
Online backup	✗
Parental controls	✓
Game mode	✓
Data protection	✓
Other features	✓

BitDefender Internet Security isn't the cheapest security suite on the market, but it gets excellent results – and, as our table shows, it does nearly everything. In addition to the regular features it also includes a safe browser, a scanner that finds unpatched programs on your system and privacy and encryption tools. The only feature you don't get is an online backup module: if you want this, you should choose the BitDefender Total Security Package instead. This costs £10 more and includes 2GB of backup space.

Details in this table are subject to change. Prices stated are from the developer's website: you may be able to save money by buying from an independent retailer.

AUTO PILOT It's a simple idea, but we haven't seen anyone else implement it so well. With Auto Pilot engaged you won't see a single popup or alert: the program will look after every aspect of your security. For hands-on control, just flick the switch.

ANTISPAM If you use a local email client, such as Windows Mail or Mozilla Thunderbird, BitDefender can protect you from spam. It doesn't work with webmail systems such as Gmail and Hotmail, however.

BitDefender's multi-tabbed settings interface gives you plenty of control over how the program works; but things are kept clear and simple, so you don't need to be a technical expert to get it working in the way you want.

If malware is found on your system, BitDefender's software will guide you through the process of deciding what to do with each threat. You can apply one action to all objects, or deal with them on a case-by-case basis.

▶ AT FIRST GLANCE, ESET SMART SECURITY MAY APPEAR INSUBSTANTIAL, BUT DON'T BE FOOLED: THERE'S A LOT GOING ON BENEATH THE SURFACE.

Eset Smart Security

SMART SECURITY'S MAIN interface is so clean and minimal that you might take it for a bare-bones program – perhaps even a free one. And the impression is backed up by a tiny memory footprint: installing Eset Smart Security adds barely more than 100MB to your system's total RAM usage. Yet beneath that super-simple front end you'll find all the important security suite features, including a firewall, a web-protection module and parental controls. What's more, you'll also find a highly efficacious malware scanner: in PC Pro's tests, Smart Security achieved one of the highest scores, protecting against 100% of malware samples while allowing 95% of legitimate applications to run without a murmur.

TEST RESULTS

100%
Malware protection score in *PC Pro*'s independent tests

95%
Legitimate software allowed to run without interruption

103MB
Added to Windows' memory usage after installation

SCORES EXPLAINED
Tests were carried out using a current version of the software during Q1 2012. The first figure reflects the software's ability to protect a test PC against an independent selection of real-world malware samples. The second indicates how many legitimate applications, again from an independent selection, ran correctly without the software interfering, raising an alert or seeking the user's permission. The third figure represents the software's overall memory footprint, as measured via the method described on p99.

COMPUTER SCAN
Click here and the main display will change to show you scanning options. Other buttons take you to the relevant settings. It's beautifully easy to find your way around.

TOOLS
Smart Security includes some useful system tools, including a file system and network activity monitor and a "snapshot" feature that can undo the damage caused by malware.

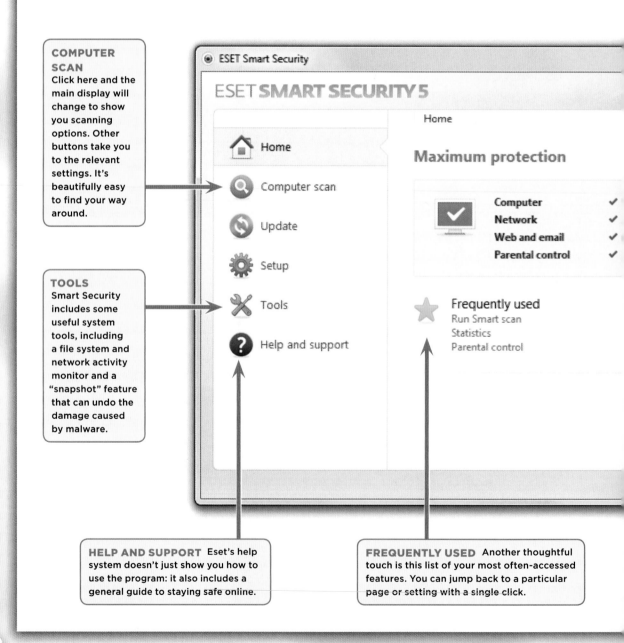

HELP AND SUPPORT Eset's help system doesn't just show you how to use the program: it also includes a general guide to staying safe online.

FREQUENTLY USED Another thoughtful touch is this list of your most often-accessed features. You can jump back to a particular page or setting with a single click.

KEY INFORMATION

SUPPORT If you have a problem or a question, you can get help by email or by phone, but be warned – the support line is a costly premium number. Unlike some of Trend Micro's competitors, the company doesn't currently give you the option to chat with a support agent online for free.

CUSTOMISE APPEARANCE
If Trend Micro's bold red interface isn't to your taste, you can switch to a different colour, or even use one of your own designs or photographs.

PARENTAL CONTROLS
The parental controls largely duplicate what you can already do with Windows, but there are reasons to prefer a third-party option, as we mention on p84.

WHERE TO GET IT	
Developer's website	www.trendmicro.co.uk
PRICING	
RRP for 1 PC (12 months)	£39.95
RRP for 3 PCs (12 months)	£49.95
Free trial available?	30 days
Windows versions supported	Windows 8, 7, Vista, XP
FEATURES	
Firewall	✗
Email scanning	✓
Web protection	✓
Anti-spam	✓
Online backup	2GB
Parental controls	✓
Game mode	✗
Data protection	✓
Other features	✓

The name's a mouthful, but there's plenty to like about Trend Micro Titanium Internet Security. Its 2GB of online backup is sufficient to protect a big folder full of important files, and security features are strong across the board – albeit those who like to fiddle with firewalls will want to look elsewhere. Factor in a perfect score in *PC Pro*'s independent malware tests, a lightweight 155MB system footprint and a very reasonable price and it's clear that Trend Micro Titanium Internet Security is a strong contender.

Details in this table are subject to change. Prices stated are from the developer's website: you may be able to save money by buying from an independent retailer.

The Security Report view breaks down the different types of threat found in an accessible format. You can easily keep track of how the dangers stack up, and see what the software's doing for you.

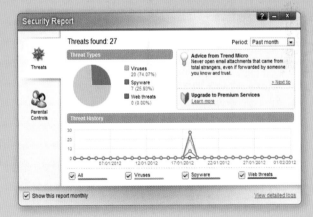

When you try to visit a dangerous site, Trend Micro steps in, placing an unmissable warning right there in your browser. If you're sure you want to continue to the site, you can click the link at the bottom of the window.

IN THIS CHAPTER

Chapter

10

PLANNING FOR

Malware is a serious threat, but it's not the only one. Computers are complex electronic systems, susceptible to any number of hardware faults. They're also expensive, making them a target for thieves. So if you want to safeguard your programs and your personal data, don't just rely on antivirus

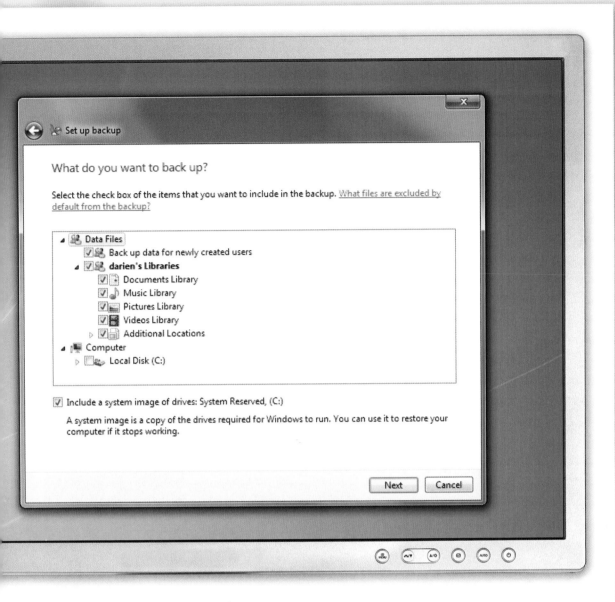

THE WORST

software: you also need to protect yourself against operating system crashes, hardware failures and physical intrusions. In this chapter we'll explain the most common disaster scenarios, and show how you can prepare for each one so as to minimise disruption and avoid losing your precious data.

What can go wrong?

SO FAR WE'VE FOCUSED on malware, and with good reason – malicious software is by far the biggest threat to the safety of your data, and the continued functioning of your PC. But if these are issues that concern you (and they surely ought to be), it's worth taking a step back and considering what else, apart from a malware attack, could go wrong.

In this chapter we'll look at some common computing disaster scenarios, besides those caused by malware, and we'll explain what you can do to mitigate the damage should any of them happen to you. Some of the advice we give is specifically directed at particular problems, but many of our tips can help protect you from data loss of any sort. So, although we're not specifically thinking about malware, you might find some of these ideas can also contribute to your anti-malware armoury.

We'll start on these pages with an overview of several types of non-malware disaster you might want to prepare for. Overleaf you'll find some suggestions of how to prepare for these eventualities; then we'll move on to address some specific issues that may arise should your PC or laptop get stolen.

HARD DISK FAILURE The most arresting potential disaster scenario is a hard disk failure. If this happens to you, you're in trouble. There's simply no way for a typical computer to revive a dead disk or rescue the data on it. If it's your system disk you can't even boot into Windows to access your programs. And if the system in question is your only device that's connected to the internet, you'll also lose access to your email accounts, social

networking, banking and so forth, until you can get back online.

When a hard disk dies it's normally because the electronics have given out – typically a component will have "blown" through overheating. If your hard disk is a traditional physical drive, which stores data on revolving platters, your data will still, technically speaking, be encoded there in magnetic form. However, recovering this data is a highly specialist job, normally carried out by forensic experts. Don't expect your high-street computer repair shop to be able to rescue your files. If you're using a solid-state disk (SSD) you're even less likely to be able to extract your files from its flash memory chips. And if you send the drive back to the manufacturer under warranty they'll send

A physical catastrophe can be as damaging as any malware.

THEFT
DOS AND DON'TS

Computers are high-value items, and laptops in particular are eminently stealable. So it's worth giving thought to the possibility of theft. Here are some tips that can ensure that, if you should have the misfortune to be a victim, your data isn't compromised.

✗ DON'T HOARD SENSITIVE DATA Most of us handle sensitive information from time to time – maybe a personal bank statement, or a financial spreadsheet for your business. If this information is saved on your computer, it'll be accessible to anyone who might pinch your PC. We're not saying that thieves will necessarily take the time to rummage through your files – it's more likely they'll just wipe the hard disk and sell the hardware on as quickly as possible. But you can't take that for granted. If you don't have a pressing need to keep a confidential document on your computer, it's safer to access it over a VPN (see below). If you do need to keep a local copy, delete it securely when you've finished with it.

✗ DON'T USE PORTABLE DRIVES USB flash drives and external drives are even easier to steal than a laptop, so avoid using them for sensitive information. They're easy to lose accidentally too: there are countless embarrassing stories of drives containing important documents being left in taxis. You don't need to be the victim of a crime to lose control of your files.

✓ DO ENCRYPT AND SHRED FILES If you must carry sensitive data on a laptop hard disk, or on a portable drive, encryption is a must. This ensures that anyone who might gain unauthorised access to your files will be unable to

read them without your password. Also, securely delete – or "shred" – files when you've finished with them, so they can't be recovered. See overleaf for a more detailed explanation of how encryption and shredding software works.

✓ DO USE A VPN We introduced VPNs – virtual private networks – on p65. Using a VPN, you can access files stored on a remote server from anywhere in the world, over a secure link. VPNs are typically used by travelling businessmen who want to connect to the office over an public network connection; but you can equally well use one to access sensitive information from your desktop PC or laptop, without ever having to store the files on your own PC. If you don't have access to a VPN you could alternatively consider using an online system such as Google Docs: if your laptop is stolen, you can simply change your password, log on from a different PC and keep working. But be aware that online services like this may not provide any legal protection against your data being leaked or lost.

✓ CONSIDER TRACKING SOFTWARE Tracking software can save the day if your laptop is stolen, potentially allowing you to track it down and recover it. It may also make it possible to remotely wipe sensitive data. See p130 for more details on tracking software.

▶ WITH A FEW FREE TOOLS, YOU CAN ENSURE THAT YOUR PRIVATE DATA WON'T FALL INTO SOMEONE ELSE'S HANDS, EVEN IF YOUR COMPUTER'S COMPROMISED OR STOLEN.

Encryption and shredding

ENCRYPTING SENSITIVE FILES is always a sensible security precaution, and it's not difficult to do – once you understand the basic principles. On these pages we'll explain how modern encryption systems work, and how file-shredding software can ensure deleted data can't be recovered.

CONTAINER ENCRYPTION The most basic encryption methods work on a file-by-file basis: when you want to protect a file, you load it into your encryption software, set a password and save the newly created encrypted version to disk. This isn't convenient for files you use regularly, however: every time you want to open an encrypted file you must run it through the decrypter, and if you make any changes you must re-encrypt the file when you're done.

Modern encryption software uses a "container" approach instead. This creates a secure virtual hard disk which you can use to store your sensitive data. The disk is, in reality, a file on your hard disk. Until you provide the encryption software with the correct password, this container file can't be accessed (it may even be invisible). But once the password is entered,

you can load, save and run files from the secure drive just as if it were a real disk or an external hard disk.

Container encryption is much more convenient than a file-by-file approach, as you only need to enter your password once per session. Indeed, if your secure volume is on an external device such as a USB flash drive, your PC can remember the password so you never need to enter it at all – though it will still be required if anyone plugs the drive into a different computer.

FULL-DISK ENCRYPTION If you want to protect a lot of files, it's possible to encrypt an entire disk, so it can't be accessed at all without the correct software and password. Encryption software that can do this is often offered with external hard disks, but you can get the same result for free with any drive using the open-source TrueCrypt encryption package – visit **www.truecrypt.org** for more details and a free download. You can even encrypt your Windows system disk: in this case, the system won't boot and the drive can't be read at all without your password, even if someone connects it to a different PC.

EXPERT TIP ▼

The technology that's used by TrueCrypt and other encryption programs is the same as that used for security certificates, as we discussed on p50. That's a huge vote of confidence in the system: if it's secure enough for the world's largest banks and retailers, it's hopefully secure enough for you.

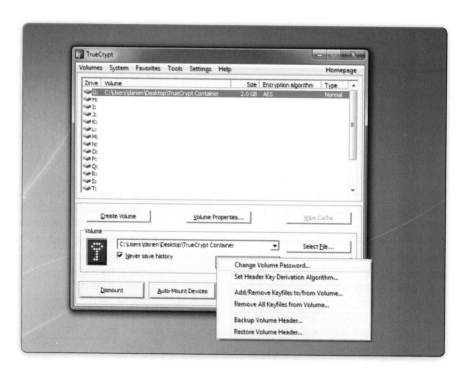

An encrypted container file appears like a virtual hard disk on your system, making it effortless to work with encrypted files.

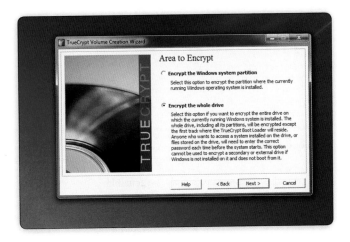

Encrypting your entire hard disk makes it impossible for anyone to access your files or even see which programs you use.

HOW ENCRYPTION WORKS Modern encryption systems use a mathematical system called the Advanced Encryption Standard, or AES. To give you an idea of just how secure this standard is, it was ratified by the US government in 2001 for use on confidential governmental business – but it's also free for you to use yourself.

The mathematics of AES are complex, but its benefits are easy to understand. Computer processors can apply AES encryption very quickly, and decrypt files just as quickly given the correct password. But trying to crack the encryption by guessing the password – a "brute force" attack – is very slow indeed. Most implementations of AES use a 256-bit encryption "key", meaning there are 2^{256} different passwords to try – or around 1.16×10^{77}. Even with the fastest computer in the world it would take literally billions of years to correctly guess a 256-bit AES password and access an encrypted container.

SENDING ENCRYPTED MAIL These types of encryption use a single password, but there's another approach too, one which uses two passwords – only one of which needs to be secret. This is called public-key encryption. Strictly speaking, this doesn't use two passwords but two keys – huge strings of numbers, typically more than 1,000 characters long. You'll be pleased to hear that these keys are generated and stored by the encryption software – you don't need to remember them yourself.

The two keys are known as the private key and the public key. Your private key must be kept secret – it might be stored in a file on your PC. But the public key is intended to be broadcast far and wide. The two keys are connected by an ingenious mathematical relationship which means that anybody can use your public key to encrypt a message – but it can then only be decrypted with the use of your private key.

It's a system that makes it easy for anyone to share information with you securely, with no need to prearrange a password. And if they send you their own public key, you can reply securely. This feature is built into many email clients, including Microsoft Outlook, and with the aid of TrueCrypt you can use public-key encryption with any email system you like.

SHREDDING UNWANTED FILES As we suggested on p127, once you've finished working with a sensitive file, it's a good idea to remove it from your system. But it's important to realise that files you delete may still be recoverable by someone determined enough. And we're not just talking about the Windows Recycle Bin – even after you've emptied this, your files aren't necessarily gone for good.

To understand why, let's take a quick look at how data is stored on a hard disk. When you save a file, its constituent ones and zeroes are written into

> *It would take literally billions of years to correctly guess a 256-bit AES password*

the next available sectors on your disk, and the details of where this data is stored are recorded into the disk's Master File Table (MFT). But when you delete that same file, the computer doesn't waste time going back and erasing all the data from each sector. It's much quicker simply to remove the file's MFT record. The sectors storing the data are now marked as unused, and may be overwritten by the next file that's saved to the disk. However, it's still possible for file-recovery software to scan the disk's sectors and read the data, assuming it hasn't been overwritten.

The solution is to overwrite deleted files yourself, ensuring they can't be recovered (this is what's meant by "shredding"). This feature isn't built into Windows, but it's included in many security suites, and there are plenty of free options – for example, try www.fileshredder.org. Some tools give you the option of overwriting deleted data multiple times, for maximum security, but practically speaking this is overkill. A single erase-and-overwrite pass will defeat all recovery attempts outside of a dedicated forensics lab.

> ! The prospect of a burglar recovering your deleted files may be alarming; but if you accidentally delete a file of your own you might be very glad it's possible to restore lost data. There are several free tools that can help: try www.recuva.com.

Tracking software

SO FAR WE'VE BEEN working on the assumption that if your computer is stolen there's nothing more you can do. But with tracking software it's possible to actively protect your data even after a theft. You might even be able to catch the thief and recover your hardware.

THE PREY PROJECT The most popular tracking software is called Prey. And the good news is, it's an open-source project, which means you can download and install it for free from www.preyproject.com. There's also a premium "Prey Pro" version which you can pay for, which supports multiple devices and extra monitoring features; but the regular free edition is adequate for most needs.

Prey works by installing a tiny, inconspicuous program on your PC that communicates regularly with Prey's central servers. If a thief steals your computer, the Prey software can quietly connect to the internet and upload useful information about its whereabouts and the thief's activity. You can also send your computer instructions to take defensive measures.

RECOVERING YOUR PC The prime goal of Prey is to help you get your PC back, so the first thing it will try to tell you is the location of your stolen computer. If possible, it works this out using nearby Wi-Fi hotspots and plots an estimated location on a map (see p141). This may sound like an imprecise approach but, in the developers' own words, it's "*shockingly* accurate".

The software can also help confirm the identity of the person who stole your PC: if it's equipped with a webcam, you can discreetly turn this on from afar, to see and record the face of whoever's sitting in front of it. You can monitor the screen too: if your thief logs into his or her email or social networking account, that gives you a strong lead which you can take to the police.

PROTECTING YOUR DATA Prey also helps ensure a thief can't access your files, even if they're not encrypted. At the click of a button, you can remotely lock down your entire operating system so an intruder can't accesss it without the password. If that seems too conspicuous, you can silently hide your email archive and wipe any stored passwords, so the thief can't get into your online accounts. If, on the other hand, you want to rattle the thief, you can trigger audio warnings and pop-up windows.

Prey isn't a perfect substitute for encrypting and shredding your files: it relies on your PC being connected to the internet, and naturally it will stop working if the thief removes or reformats the hard disk. But since it's free, you've nothing to lose by installing Prey as an extra precaution against theft.

EXPERT TIP ▼

Prey isn't the only anti-theft system around. Businesses might want to consider Intel's vPro remote management technology, which includes many of the same tracking features as Prey. Because vPro is a hardware feature, it's impossible for a thief to circumvent, even if he wipes the hard disk.

Prey lets you collect information from your PC, and perform various actions, after it's stolen.

IN THIS CHAPTER

Chapter

11

MOBILE PHONES

Not many years ago, the idea of a phone catching a virus seemed laughable. But modern smartphones and tablets are computers in their own right – and that means they're as vulnerable to the tricks and scams of cybercriminals as any desktop PC. In this final chapter we explore the dangers that lurk in

AND TABLETS

wait for smartphone and tablet users. We'll describe the threats, show you the warning signs to watch for, and introduce the mobile security software that can keep you safe. We'll also look at mobile tracking software, which can help you recover your phone or tablet should a thief make off with it.

Mobile device dangers

THE PAST FIVE OR TEN years have seen a revolution in our pockets. Simple, functional mobile phones have been replaced with powerful smartphones, capable of browsing the web, sending and receiving email, watching videos online, playing games – and even installing new programs, or "apps" as they're commonly called. More recently we've seen the rise of tablets too – most visibly the Apple iPad, but also any number of alternatives running Google's rival Android operating system.

These versatile mobile devices are, to all intents and purposes, computers. They don't run Windows, and they don't have keyboards and mice; but fundamentally they're capable of doing all the same sorts of task. And that means they're every bit as vulnerable to online dangers as a regular PC.

We should be clear that we mean this in a general sense. There's no reason why a virus or Trojan couldn't attack Android or Apple's iOS; but existing malware, designed to target Windows and popular desktop browsers, won't itself be able to infect an mobile device. For an exploit to work, it must be tailored to a particular operating system

or application. So far, touch wood, such malware has been quite thin on the ground – though, as we'll explain on p136, it's a bad idea to let your guard down, especially if you're an Android fan.

But as we've explained in previous chapters, malware isn't the only online hazard out there – and in some ways smartphones and tablets are even more at risk than PCs.

POTENTIAL FOR PHISHING Mobile web browsers typically use simpler interfaces than their desktop counterparts, and on smartphones in particular they're designed to be more compact. This means there's space for less information to be displayed – and this can be dangerous.

For example, let's say someone sends you a phishing email. On a desktop browser you can easily check where the main link goes by hovering the mouse over it. In a mobile browser that option isn't normally available, or isn't so easy to access. So you click blindly on the link – and find yourself directed to **www.personalbanking.com.34host.cn**. As we mentioned in our discussion of phishing in Chapter 2,

Scanning a QR code could lead you anywhere on the web – and there's no way to look before you leap.

this is a highly suspicious address. But if you're using a mobile browser with a small display, there's a good chance it won't all fit on the screen. What you see will be something like "www.personalbanking.com..." – an address that's much less likely to arouse suspicion.

Another potential red flag for phishing that we discussed in Chapter 2 was the absence of a security certificate. This applies to mobile platforms just as much to "real" PCs – but because of the compact designs of mobile browsers, the display of certificate information may be much less conspicuous, or it might not be shown at all. Once again, it's much easier to be taken in on a mobile platform than on a regular desktop PC or laptop.

WAYS TO BE WAYLAID An additional danger with mobile platforms is that there are more ways to end up on a scam site. If you're using a smartphone, phishers can send you SMS text messages containing dodgy links, as well as the more common emails. A message sent via SMS is much more likely to reach you, as few mobile phone operators do much to block text message "spam" in the way email providers do. Because text messages are necessarily short and simple, there may be no giveaway clues that the message isn't legitimate. And, because it comes via a more personal medium, you may be more likely to trust it.

You could also end up on a malicious website if you make a habit of scanning QR codes. These black and white codes – as shown in the image opposite – often contain web links that you can visit by simply pointing your smartphone at them (assuming you've installed a free barcode-reading app). QR codes are popularly printed on advertisements and documents, to help people easily find more information online.

Unfortunately, when you scan a QR code you have no way of knowing where it's going to lead you. Your barcode-reading app might show the address before opening the browser, but you can't always identify a dangerous website from its address. Even an apparently legitimate poster could lead you to a scam site: it's easy for a malicious person to stick their own QR codes over the official ones, and very difficult to spot at a glance.

When you're using a mobile browser, it can be difficult to confirm the authenticity of a website.

In some ways smartphones and tablets are even more at risk than PCs

THEFT Mobile phone theft is an unfortunate fact of life. And because we use modern smartphones to do so much, a stolen phone can have far more serious consequences than simply having to change your number. If a thief can use your phone to access your email, he has immediate access to all sorts of personal information about you. If he's enterprising, he can also go onto websites you use and reset your password. He may be able to view your calendar, and see when you're away from home. If you're using a file-syncing app like Dropbox, he could access your personal files. And having possession of your phone even allows him to defeat the mobile security code systems used by some banks (see p47).

If all this sounds alarming, there's no need to panic. As with laptop theft, the odds are that your thief will wipe the phone, to erase his tracks. And as soon as you report the phone stolen, its network access will be cut off. Nevertheless, it's clear that the worst case scenario is quite damaging indeed. Again, as with laptop theft, it's worth considering some type of tracking software – see p140.

> When you upgrade your mobile phone, the old one might still contain personal information. It's a good idea to perform a factory reset before selling it on or disposing of it – or, indeed, before leaving it languishing in a drawer.

▶ BEFORE YOU DOWNLOAD YOUR NEXT APP, STOP TO THINK – IS IT POSSIBLE THAT YOU MIGHT BE INSTALLING A TROJAN ON YOUR SMARTPHONE OR TABLET?

The dangers of malicious apps

INSTALLING APPS IS part of the fun of owning a smartphone or a tablet. And with so many games and tools available at pocket-money prices (and even for free) it's tempting to download dozens of them. Unfortunately, if you're a voracious installer, you could end up unwittingly installing a malicious app.

Malicious apps present themselves as something useful or desirable, but they have an ulterior purpose. In other words, they're Trojans that attack mobile devices. Sometimes a malicious app will be written from scratch, but often the authors will add malware to a popular existing app, and try to trick you into installing this "Trojanised" package rather than the official one.

It's a scam that can be hard to spot. The mobile app market is such a vibrant place that new publishers come and go on an almost daily basis. Innocent downloaders are therefore unlikely to check or recognise if a program is being distributed by the wrong publisher – whereas you'd probably be suspicious if you saw a well-known desktop application like Word or Photoshop being offered under the wrong company's name!

WHO'S AT RISK? Technically speaking, all types of smartphones and tablets are vulnerable to malicious apps. If it's possible to install *bona fide* apps, it's equally possible to install malevolent ones.

In practice, however, some platforms are safer than others. Apple's iOS devices – the iPod Touch, iPhone and iPad – are strictly locked down, so that apps can be installed only from the iTunes App Store; and before an app can be offered there it must be tested by Apple's own technicians. This means malware is likely to be spotted and rejected, without ever being offered for download. And if a malicious app does somehow slip through the net, it can be yanked out of the App Store as soon as its dangerous intent is discovered, minimising the chances of your installing something nasty.

Things are much less rosy for Android users. Although Google offers a central store for finding and downloading Android apps – branded "Google Play" – it's open to everyone, with no requirement for apps to be tested or approved. This means that, although your download may appear to come from an official source, it could easily be a Trojan. In principle, Google has

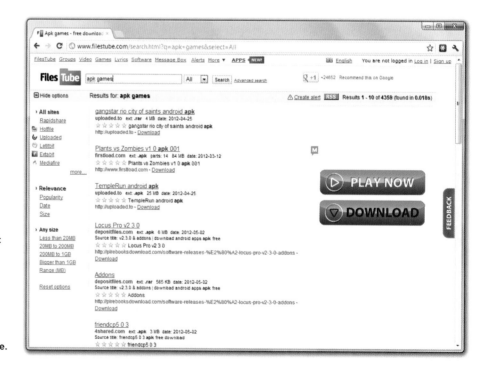

Sites that offer Android APKs for direct download – including pirated copies of commercial apps – are a breeding ground for mobile malware.

A malicious app could run up your phone bill, and incur unexpected mobile data charges.

the power to remove apps from Google Play once their malicious nature is brought to its attention, but in practice malware has been known to remain available on the site for many months.

The best protection Google Play does offer is a user reviews system: if you can see that tens of thousands of people before you have installed an app, and given it high ratings, it's unlikely to be malware – though of course its malicious functions could merely be so well concealed that they haven't been noticed.

Android also lets you install applications from outside of Google Play – enabling this is a simple matter of ticking a box in the settings on your phone or tablet. And there are plenty of websites offering free APK files – that is, Android app installation files – for you to download, often including pirated copies of popular paid-for apps. The trouble is, when you download a file from a site like this, you have no indication whatsoever of its provenance, nor do you get the reassurance of a review system. This means sites like these can be used for spreading malware, or as the destination for a phishing campaign. In all, we suggest you steer well clear. (This also applies if you're using an iPhone that's been "jailbroken" – that is, hacked to permit the installation of apps from sources other than the App Store.)

If you're using a mobile operating system other than iOS or Android – perhaps Windows Phone, or RIM's BlackBerry OS – there's still a risk from malicious apps, but it's probably small. Since these platforms have far fewer users than the "big two", there's less to be gained from targeting them.

WHAT'S THE DANGER? A modern mobile device with an internet connection can do anything a desktop PC can do – which means malware can do all the same things too.

We mentioned back on p57 that one of the lesser effects of malware – though still a serious concern – is its propensity for clogging up your network by consuming lots of bandwidth. On a mobile device this is a more urgent issue, because it's quite likely you're paying for your data connection on a per-megabyte basis. Simply by attempting to spread, or by contacting a home server, the malware could be running up a hefty data bill.

Some mobile malware can also incur charges deliberately. On p11 we described a class of Trojan known as "dialers": these attempt to use your modem to surreptitiously dial premium numbers, so the Trojan author profits at your expense. Dialers had their heyday in the early 2000s, when dial-up internet

Google Play is open to everyone, with no requirement for apps to be tested or approved

access was the norm. As homes have switched to broadband, dialers have all but died out on the desktop. But now people are starting to use mobile phones to access the internet, the idea has gained a new lease of life. Researchers have identified a widespread mobile malware scam known as "RuFraud", which silently sends repeated messages to premium SMS services, costing you several pounds every time. If your tablet only has a Wi-Fi connection then obviously it's safe, but for smartphone users it's a very real threat.

Mobile malware can also steal information in just the same way as desktop malware, perhaps sending stored passwords and information copied from email back to its creator. Though it's not yet widespread, we've also heard of malware creators attempting to set up mobile botnets (see p60) which could prove very insidious and difficult to shut down.

Happily, there are steps you can take to protect yourself. Overleaf, we'll show you some warning signs to look out for, and we'll take a look at the mobile security software that can keep you safe.

> ! Google Play isn't the only app store on Android – many device manufacturers offer branded stores, and Amazon has its own app store in the US. Check what security measures are in place before downloading from a third-party store.

▶ MOBILE MALWARE PROBABLY WON'T POP UP A HELPFUL MESSAGE TO TELL YOU IT'S THERE – BUT IF YOU KEEP YOUR EYES PEELED YOU MAY SPOT ITS PRESENCE.

Mobile security warning signs

Keep an eye on the permissions apps ask for when you install them – these can be a clue to their true natures.

THE BEST WAY TO protect yourself against malicious apps is to install mobile security software that can positively identify threats – as we discuss opposite. However, whether or not you're using such software, there are also some general warning signs to look out for, which could tip you off that an app isn't what it claims to be.

EXCESSIVE PERMISSIONS Whenever you install an Android app, you're required to explicitly grant it any permissions it requires. These might typically include the ability to access your personal information, the ability to detect your location – and the ability to access "services that cost you money".

It's always a good idea to check over an app's permissions before installing it, and to ask yourself whether they seem reasonable. For example, a camera app might have a valid reason for sending picture messages. But there's no reason why a simple game would need that ability. If an app asks for a suspicious set of powers, we suggest you cancel the installation – or at least investigate why before proceeding.

UNEXPECTED ROOT If you've "rooted" your device – that is, broken the manufacturer's software protection – then you may find some apps unexpectedly ask for root access. If you grant it, the app will be able to do absolutely anything it likes on your system. Be wary of apps that request this without giving a very good reason.

CHECK YOUR BILLS Keep an eye on your mobile phone bills and data usage. If you start seeing charges you don't recognise, or if your data usage suddenly rockets for no apparent reason, it could indicate that a malicious app is operating on your phone without your knowledge.

STRANGE BEHAVIOUR Sometimes the only clue you'll get is that your phone doesn't behave quite as it should: for example, when you turn on the screen, you might see a different app to the one you were expecting. This doesn't prove anything in itself, but it could be a sign that it's time to test drive some mobile security software.

INTRODUCING MOBILE SECURITY SUITES

If you're a worried Android user, there are many mobile security suites that can protect you against malicious apps and other invasions of your privacy and security. Often, these are made by the same companies as desktop suites: below you'll see sample screens from AVG, Norton and Kaspersky's products. But there are other dedicated mobile developers too, such as Lookout Mobile Security.

Most mobile security software comes in a basic free edition, available via Google Play, which will protect you from malware. For more features, you can upgrade to a paid-for licence. Here's a guide to some of the features on offer.

✓ **ANTI-THEFT** As we mentioned on p135, mobile phones get stolen. Common anti-theft features include the ability to remotely lock or wipe the phone, to ensure a thief can't access your personal data. You can even configure a message to be displayed on the screen if your phone is reported stolen, to help you get it back.

✓ **PRIVACY PROTECTION** If you don't want your contacts and communciations to fall into the wrong hands, it's often possible to hide your address book, message history and calls. Once you've done this, no one else who may gain access to your phone will be able to discover who you've been calling, or what information you've been sharing over SMS.

✓ **ENCRYPTION** If you're storing sensitive files on your phone or tablet, encryption ensures they can't be accessed without the correct password. Even if the data is stored on an external memory card, its contents will be securely concealed from prying eyes.

✓ **ANTI-SPAM** SMS spam is a nuisance – and, as we've noted, it can be a vector for phishing attempts, making it a security concern too. Mobile security software can intercept messages (and phone calls too) and automatically accept or reject them based on your criteria, ensuring only people you want to hear from can reach you.

✓ **PARENTAL CONTROLS** If your child has a smartphone, he or she may have the ability not only to visit inappropriate sites, but to download malware and to access costly premium rate services. Mobile parental controls may be the answer, allowing you to lock down their network access.

✓ **TRACKING** Many mobile security suites also include tracking features, which can be used to locate your phone if it's stolen. Or, if the phone is being used by a child, you can use these features to check on their whereabouts. We'll discuss this in more depth on the following pages.

> ⓘ We focus on Android here because it's the mobile platform that has the most malware – and the most security suites. But there's plenty of security software for other mobile platforms too: a quick web search will show you some options.

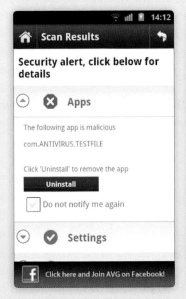

THE ULTIMATE GUIDE TO INTERNET SECURITY

▶ IF YOUR SHINY SMARTPHONE OR EXPENSIVE TABLET GOES WALKABOUT, DON'T GIVE UP HOPE – WITH THE RIGHT SOFTWARE IT MAY WELL BE POSSIBLE TO TRACK IT DOWN.

Apple's iCloud service includes an easy-to-use "Find my iPhone" feature

Mobile tracking software

AS WE'VE NOTED, mobile phones – and snazzy internet tablets – have an unfortunate tendency to get stolen. But with the right software installed, your purloined hardware can "phone home", and feed back a wealth of information that could help you to recover it. Alternatively, if data security is your greatest concern, you can prime your mobile devices to wipe themselves clean as soon as they check in to the internet. We've already looked at software that works in this way on laptops and desktop PCs (see p130); now let's explore your options for mobile devices.

FIND MY IPHONE Apple's iPhones and iPads come with tracking and remote-wiping capabilities built in to the operating system – and it's free to use. The only proviso is that you have to sign up for Apple's free iCloud service, as this is how you access the feature. You'll be asked whether you want to enable "Find my iPhone" or "Find my iPad" when you first set up an iPhone or iPad. If you don't do this at the time, you can enable it later via your device's settings menu.

Once you've enabled the service, you can track a lost device by simply logging into www.icloud.com and clicking on Find my iPhone. Your device's location will be displayed directly in your browser, as above. How precise this is depends on what sort of device you're using: an iPhone with built-in GPS can use satellite positioning to give a very accurate reading indeed. A Wi-Fi based iPad will have to resort to other methods, and may give a less exact report of its location – see the panel opposite for a guide to how mobile devices can find their own location.

Once your device has appeared on the map, you can click the blue Information icon for more options, including pushing a message to your device, locking it remotely (if you have a PIN code set up) – and the nuclear option, wiping it remotely.

Since Find my iPhone is a software service, it isn't bulletproof: it will stop working if your device is wiped and paired with a new iTunes account. So your chances of tracking down and recovering your device are higher the faster you act.

EXPERT TIP ▾

GPS relies on your phone being able to receive transmissions from at least three satellites, so it needs to be outdoors or near a window. If it's being kept in a basement, or driven around in the boot of a car, it will have to fall back to less precise methods of geolocation.

WHERE'S MY PHONE?

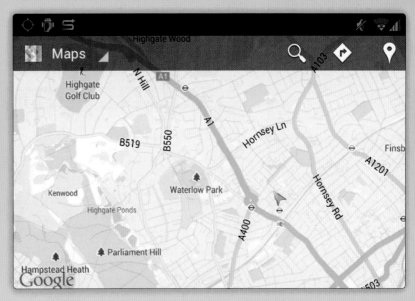

TRACKING AN ANDROID DEVICE If you're using an Android phone or tablet, you probably won't have any pre-installed anti-theft software. This isn't a problem: there are plenty of options you can install yourself. This includes a good number of integrated mobile security suites, such as those we've already mentioned on p139. But you may be able to save money by looking outside of the big brands.

One obvious place to start looking is the Prey software, which we described on p130 as a powerful antidote to laptop theft. This software isn't just for PCs: it's also offered in a native Android version. You'll find it available for download in Google Play.

Prey provides all the location tracking, phone locking and alarm services you could ask for – and it can track the technical details of any networks your phone's accessing too. If you suspect your phone's been stolen, you can send it a text to remotely activate Prey and begin tracking your device, so you don't need to keep the app running and consuming battery power until you need it. If you've rooted your phone, you can also allow the app to use root privileges to hide itself, ensuring it can't be uninstalled by more tech-savvy thieves.

The best bit is that Prey for Android is, like the PC version, completely free. So there's no good reason not to install it – unless, that is, you're using a different tracking system.

PROTECTION AFTER THE FACT If your Android phone is stolen and you haven't installed any tracking software, you might assume it's lost for good. But don't give up just yet: Google Play allows you to install apps on your Android devices remotely, via the web browser on your PC. So as long as the thief doesn't log your device out of your Google account, you can actually load tracking software onto it *after* it's stolen. A tracking app called Plan B is designed for precisely this eventuality: it installs silently, and sends regular updates of your phone's location. To find it, search Google Play for "Plan B", published by Lookout Mobile Security.

Many phones and tablets have built-in GPS chips. This makes locating a lost or stolen device a snip. Using GPS satellite signals, a mobile device can triangulate its own position to a very high degree of accuracy – typically to within a few metres. When this information is relayed back to you, you can work out exactly where your phone is, right down to which room in a building it's in.

Phones without GPS can use Google's location API. This makes use of data gathered by Google's Street View cars, which includes the locations of wireless base stations. By checking which base stations it can see, your device can work out where it is.

If there are no base stations around, a mobile device can analyse where its own internet address is registered. This is an imprecise approach, though: it may pin the device's location down only to an area of a few square miles.

Security jargon explained

ADMINISTRATOR ACCOUNT An account on a Windows PC that has the power to change system settings and install programs.

ADWARE Malware that inserts adverts into web pages or elsewhere. Also, legitimate software that displays adverts within its interface.

ANTIVIRUS A general term for software that protects against malware, but also used specifically to refer to security software that doesn't include a firewall or other features. See also *security suite*.

AUTOPLAY A system in Windows that automatically runs a program, or performs some other action, when an optical disc or USB drive is connected.

BEHAVIOURAL DETECTION An approach to identifying malware based on analysing what it does, rather than relying on signatures.

BITTORRENT A software-sharing system commonly used for distributing pirated software and media files – and for spreading Trojans.

BOOT CD A disc you can use to start your PC and perform system repairs, scan for viruses etc. if you're unable to boot from your hard disk for any reason.

BOTNET A network of computers that have been infected with malware which enables them to be remotely controlled without the owner's knowledge.

CYBER-BULLYING Taunting or teasing using electronic media, such as text messages or Facebook wall posts.

DIALER A type of malware that surreptitiously dials premium-rate telephone services from a modem, making money for the owner of the service and racking up large bills for the unwitting victim.

DENIAL OF SERVICE ATTACK An attack that shuts down a server by flooding it with connection requests. When a large number of computers are used to send traffic from many directions at once, this is called a Distributed Denial of Service Attack.

DOMAIN NAME A "base" internet address, such as amazon.com or hsbc.co.uk. Addresses within this domain, such as www.amazon.com or personalbanking.hsbc.co.uk, are called subdomains.

DRIVE-BY DOWNLOAD A type of attack in which a website attempts to download and install malware automatically through your browser.

EVIL TWIN ATTACK A trick where a malicious person tries to trick you into connecting to an unsafe wireless network by giving it an identical or very similar SSID to a legitimate network nearby.

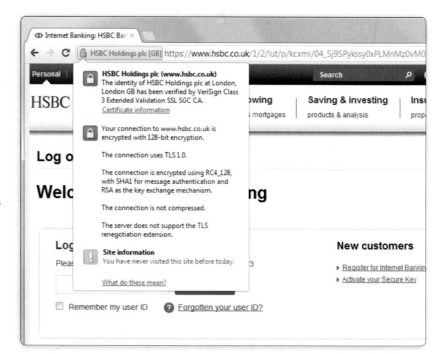

EXPERT TIP ▼

If you crave more information about any of these topics – or if you've come across a term that isn't defined here – try a web search, or visit an online resource such as Wikipedia (http://en.wikipedia.org). There's a huge amount of helpful and accessible information on offer for free.

EXPLOIT A security loophole in an operating system or program that can be used to spread malware.

EXTENDED VALIDATION (EV) CERTIFICATE The most trustworthy type of security certificate, granted to an organisation only after it has been thoroughly vetted. When you visit a site with an EV certificate you will normally see its details appear in a green box in or next to the address bar of your browser. You can click on this box for more information (pictured opposite).

FIREWALL A software or hardware system that monitors all incoming network connections and only permits those deemed safe, either by you or by an automatic rule. A two-way firewall monitors outgoing connections as well.

GAME MODE (ALSO MOVIE MODE) A mode in which security software suppresses all pop-ups and makes decisions automatically, so as not to interrupt while you're playing a game or watching a movie.

GEOLOCATION The process of determining the physical location of an electronic device – which can be very useful when a laptop or smartphone is stolen.

GPS The Global Positioning System, a satellite-based system which compatible devices can use to locate themselves to a very high degree of precision – so long as they can "see" the sky.

HTTPS A secure web browsing protocol: if your address bar shows an "HTTPS" conneciton, your communications with the site you're visiting can't be spied on or intercepted. If you only see "HTTP", the connection isn't secure.

IPV4 / IPV6 IPv4 is the existing system of network addressing, which provides a degree of protection against worms. The newer IPv6 system, which is slowly replacing it, offers no such built-in protection.

KEY LOGGER A type of malware that secretly monitors your key strokes and reports them back to its creator, in the hope of capturing login details, passwords or other sensitive information.

MAC ADDRESS Short for Media Access Control address: a unique code that identifies a physical device. You can prevent unauthorised people from connecting to your wireless network by restricting access to the MAC addresses of devices you know and recognise.

MACRO VIRUS A type of virus which operates within a macro scripting language hosted by another application. Microsoft Office has historically been a common target for macro viruses, but in recent years its security has been upgraded to prevent this.

MASTER FILE TABLE (MFT) The record on a disk of which data relates to which file, and where it's stored. When a file is deleted it will be removed from the MFT, but the data may remain physically on the disk, and could be recovered with the right software – hence the need for shredding software.

NETWORK LOCATION A setting in Windows which lets you categorise a network as Home, Work or Public. Depending on the category you choose for a network, different sharing and firewall settings will be applied by default.

PARENTAL CONTROLS Software that restricts the amount of time a child can spend online, the types of website they can visit and other aspects of their computer use. In a few cases parental controls are also built into a router.

PASSWORD MANAGER Software that remembers passwords for you, and which can automatically log you into websites and services at the click of a button, defeating key loggers.

PAYLOAD The functional aspect of a piece of malware, as opposed to its distribution mechanism. Typically a payload might involve deleting files, stealing information or subsuming a PC into a botnet.

PERSONAL INFORMATION MONITOR A system that monitors outgoing information from your PC and alerts you if certain data – such as credit card numbers or addresses – are being transmitted.

PHISHING Attempting to trick users into giving up account details and passwords by creating fake websites, which are typically advertised through sending fake email or SMS messages.

RANSOMWARE Malware that encrypts files, or causes some other inconvenience, and demands payment before the inconvenience will be lifted.

SAFE MODE A special troubleshooting mode in which you can start up Windows, where only a minimal set of drivers and programs is loaded.

SANDBOX A simulated, virtual environment in which you or a security suite can test out an unknown application without giving it access to your personal files or your network connection.

SCREEN SNIFFER A type of malware that monitors what's being displayed on your screen, hoping to capture sensitive information.

SECURITY CERTIFICATE A digital code which confirms the identity of the website you're visiting, and which can be used to encrypt your communications with it.

SECURITY SUITE An integrated package that contains antivirus software plus additional features such as a firewall and parental controls.

SHOULDER SURFING Obtaining unauthorised information by watching over someone's shoulder (or from some other vantage point) while they're using a computer in a public place.

SHREDDING Securely deleting files from a hard disk so that they can't be recovered, even with specialist software.

SIGNATURE A distinctive snippet of code which can be used to positively identify a particular item of malware.

SITEKEY A security system designed to prove the authenticity of a website by showing you a secret image and phrase, known only to you and the real bank or merchant.

SPYWARE A term commonly (and misleadingly) used for quasi-legal software that hijacks your web browsing experience – for example, by changing your settings and showing adverts.

SSID Short for Service Set ID: the name of a wireless network. When you buy a wireless router the SSID is often set to the manufacturer's name: you can change this to whatever you like to identify your network.

STANDARD ACCOUNT An account on a Windows PC that has only limited abilities to change system settings and install software.

SYSTEM RESTORE A feature in Windows that allows you to "roll back" recent changes, and which can undo some of the damage caused by an infection.

TAN (TRANSACTION AUTHENTICATION NUMBER) A system whereby the customer confirms an online transaction is legitimate by providing a secret one-time authentication number, as supplied by his or her bank.

TRACKING COOKIES Tiny bits of information stored on your PC when you visit websites. These can store login details and other personal data, and they

---

> Computing is a fast-moving industry, and online criminals are always trying to stay one step ahead – so new issues and new jargon are constantly appearing. One of the best ways to stay informed is to follow technology news sites like www.pcpro.co.uk.

can also be used by advertisers to track what sort of products you might be interested in.

TRACKING SOFTWARE Systems such as Prey or Find My iPhone which enable you to locate and remotely take control of an internet-connected device if it's been lost or stolen.

TROJAN A form of malware that tricks you (or your computer) into downloading and installing it, either by masquerading as legitimate software or by making use of an exploit.

UNIVERSAL PLUG 'N' PLAY (UPNP) A system that allows software to configure your router automatically as needed. This makes setting up new network applications easy, but it could be a loophole for malware.

USER ACCOUNT CONTROL (UAC) A system in Windows that requires permission from an Administrator before important system settings can be changed.

VIRTUAL PRIVATE NETWORK (VPN) An encrypted connection that lets you access a secure server over the internet without any danger of your connection being spied upon.

VIRUS Strictly speaking, malware that spreads by making copies of its own code. More loosely, though, the term is commonly used to mean malware of any type (as in *antivirus*).

WEB SCANNING Monitoring the websites you visit and giving warnings when you're in danger of winding up on a fake site, or one with a known history of serving malware.

WEP Short for Wired Equivalent Privacy: an encryption system used by older wireless devices. Now deprecated in favour of WPA2 after a security weakness was found.

WORM A type of malware that spreads directly across a network, or over the internet.

WPA2 Short for Wi-Fi Protected Access: a password-based security system that prevents unauthorised devices from joining a wireless network.

ZERO-DAY When describing a malware attack, "zero-day" means the attack makes use of an exploit not previously known to researchers – so there has been no opportunity to patch it.

THE ULTIMATE GUIDE TO INTERNET SECURITY

EDITORIAL

Author & Designer
Darien Graham-Smith
darien@pcpro.co.uk

Photo credit
Lise Smith (photo of author, p3)

Editorial Director
Tim Danton
timdanton@dennis.co.uk

Sub Editor
Julie Birrell

LICENSING & SYNDICATION

International Licensing
Carlotta Serantoni
carlotta_serantoni@dennis.co.uk
+44 (0)20 7907 6314

Syndication
Anj Dosaj-Halai
anj_dosaj-halai@dennis.co.uk
+44 (0)20 7907 6132

ADVERTISING & MARKETING

MagBook Account Manager
Katie Wood +44 (0)7971 937162

Senior MagBook Executive
Matt Wakefield +44 (0)20 7907 6617

MagBook Publisher
Dharmesh Mistry +44 (0)20 7907 6100

Marketing Executive
Paul Goodhead +44 (0)20 7907 6012

MANAGEMENT

Group Managing Director
Ian Westwood

Managing Director
John Garewal

Deputy Managing Director
Tim Danton

Newstrade Director
David Barker

Chief Operating Officer
Brett Reynolds

Group Finance Director
Ian Leggett

Chief Executive
James Tye

Chairman
Felix Dennis

MAGBOOK

The "MagBook" brand is a trademark of Dennis Publishing Ltd, 30 Cleveland St, London W1T 4JD. Company registered in England. All material © Dennis Publishing Ltd, licensed by Felden 2012, and may not be reproduced in whole or part without the consent of the publishers.
The Ultimate Guide to Internet Security
ISBN 1-78106-026-6

Printed by
BGP, Bicester, Oxfordshire

Liability
While every care was taken during the preparation of this MagBook, the publishers cannot be held responsible for the accuracy of the information or any consequence arising. All judgements are based on products available to us at the time. "Value for money" comments are based on current UK prices. Dennis Publishing takes no responsibility for the content of any external websites mentioned.

The paper used within this MagBook is produced from sustainable fibre, manufactured by mills with a valid chain of custody.

Index